THE MAGIC OF KRISHNA

THE MAGIC OF KRISHNA

SWARNESH SINHA

Sarvatra
An imprint of Manjul Publishing House

Sarvatra
An imprint of Manjul Publishing House
• 2nd Floor, Usha Preet Complex,
42 Malviya Nagar, Bhopal 462 003 - India
• C-16, Sector 3, Noida, Uttar Pradesh 201301, India
Website: www.manjulindia.com

The Magic of Krishna by Swarnesh Sinha

This edition first published in 2025
Third impression 2026

ISBN 978-93-5543-606-1

Printed and bound in India by Repro India Ltd.

To the glory of the Supreme Lord,

Shri Krishna

In Praise of The Magic of Krishna...

A truly remarkable story about courage and faith

Mr Sinha is a gifted writer who not only has a way with words — the lyrical elegance of his prose, the choice of words, the subtle humour — but also has a great understanding of life. He has deftly woven a modern tale against a mythical backdrop but with a twist. In the Mahabharata, the war is fought on a physical battlefield but here, the war is within, an inner war against fear that assumes monstrous proportions. The hero has to fight a longish, brutish battle before emerging victorious with the blessings of both Lord Hanuman and Lord Krishna. A truly remarkable story about courage and faith that I will remember for a long time!

—Pravin Bakshi, IAS

A Profound and Uplifting Journey – A Must-Read!

'The Magic of Krishna' by Swarnesh Sinha is more than just a novel—it is a deeply moving exploration of faith, resilience, and the unseen forces that shape our lives. With a masterful blend of spirituality and human struggle, this book takes readers on a journey of self-discovery, proving that even in our darkest moments, divine guidance is always present. Through its richly woven narrative, it offers a compelling reflection on the battles we all face—doubt, fear, ambition, and the search for purpose. At its heart, it is a reminder that surrendering to faith does not mean giving up control, but rather finding the courage to walk the path meant for us.

Swarnesh Sinha's storytelling is immersive and profound, drawing from a wealth of experience in shaping young minds and understanding the complexities of human potential. His ability to intertwine the wisdom of the Mahabharata with modern life makes 'The Magic of Krishna' both timeless and incredibly relevant. This book is for anyone who has ever felt lost, anyone who seeks inspiration, and anyone who believes in the power of transformation. It is a beacon of hope, a call to trust in the divine, and a testament to the fact that life's greatest struggles often lead to its most extraordinary blessings.

—Adit Bhansali, alumnus,
Princeton University, USA

Masterpiece!

'The Magic of Krishna' is a profound and inspiring read, one I would recommend to everyone. It weaves a powerful narrative about confronting Fear and drawing strength from unwavering faith in oneself, guided by the wisdom of Lord Krishna. What sets this book apart is its seamless and flowing writing style. Mr Sinha's storytelling feels organic and effortless, reminiscent of great authors like Toni Morrison, the Nobel laureate, who also writes with natural grace. The narrative is beautifully written, and every word feels perfectly placed, making it hard to imagine the story told in any other way.

In addition to its artistic brilliance, the book imparts priceless life lessons, offering inspiration and empowerment to its readers. In fact, Mr. Sinha captures these lessons akin to the renowned Paulo Coelho. His ability to convey profound insights with clarity sets this book apart.

This masterpiece is more than just a story—it's an experience that leaves you uplifted. I am grateful to have read it and am sure it will resonate with many others. It's a must-read for anyone seeking inspiration and strength in the face of life's challenges.

—Siddhant Sanghi, alumnus,
Columbia University, USA

Spellbinding!

I must say that this book is a masterpiece. It is for everyone to read because it tells you to face your fears and never give up. The emotions and struggles that the author went through and overcame will make everyone believe that nothing is impossible to achieve and God is there to slowly and steadily take us out of the thunderstorms that wobble our path to glory. Amazing read not only for someone distressed but for every one of us. I am sure it's going to be one of the bestsellers. Hare Krishna!

—Bhuvan Trikha, Australia

Heartfelt and Inspiring!

I just finished reading the book, and I must say that it's truly inspiring and heartfelt. The book is a candid account of the struggles Arjun faces in life, and how he finds solace and guidance in the teachings of Lord Krishna and Hanuman Ji.

What struck me most about the book is its honesty and vulnerability. You have shared the innermost thoughts and feelings of the protagonist and have spoken about the challenges he faced in his personal and professional life. Your writing is simple, yet powerful, and it's clear that you have poured your heart and soul into this book.

One of the things that I appreciated most about the book is the way you have woven the story with the teachings of Lord Krishna and Hanuman Ji. You have drawn inspiration from their lives and teachings and have applied those lessons to Arjun's life. It's clear that their guidance has been a source of strength and comfort for you, and you have shared that inspiration with your readers.

Overall, I would highly recommend this book to anyone who is looking for an inspiring and uplifting story, a testament to the power of faith, perseverance, and family, and it's a reminder that we all have the strength and resilience to overcome any challenges that come our way.

—Dharmendra Sinha

A poignant saga of thwarted aspirations and ultimate redemption

Swarnesh Sinha is a storyteller writing from the heart. He weaves an interesting tale about a gifted kid who falters at crucial junctures due to baseless fears but ultimately finds deliverance at the hands of Lord Krishna. His prose, I must say, is distinguished not only by heart-wrenching pathos reminiscent of Hardy but also by a strong element of positivity and hope, showing his deep spiritual connection. Yes, it is rather personalised, but so are most of the emotional writings.

—C K Mishra, IAS (Retired)

Captivating!

The 'Magic of Krishna' is a captivating story of a young boy, Arjun, from Patna. The book gives very meaningful insights into

Arjun's train of thoughts, aspirations, struggles, frustrations and adjustments he had to make to survive with dignity in this good, bad, and ugly world. The story gives a vivid description of the effects of fear Arjun had to go through. The reader is taken through the details of the family milieu, Arjun's relationship with his parents and siblings, and the financial struggles of the family. Arjun's failed aspirations to become an IAS officer and then later, to become a movie star, the stress, strains, and emotional upheaval endured, have all been aptly depicted and are very interesting to read. The narration of finally falling in love, getting married to a supportive wife, and initially being under acute financial squeeze after his marriage, forcing him to stay with his in-laws in Mumbai, has a touch of realism.

The reader is also taken through a labyrinth of issues that crop up due to the acute emotional stress faced by Arjun and his wife. How Arjun's faith in Lord Hanuman and Lord Krishna helps him to surmount most of his problems in life and he finally becomes successful and settled, has been woven into a great story.

Swarnesh Sinha has special writing skills which make the reader keen to read the book in one go.'The Magic of Krishna' is quite a commendable feat!

—Vimal Kirti Singh, IAS (voluntarily retired),
Advocate, Supreme Court

CHAPTER ONE

I'm fifteen years old, and I bet it's not very often that you come across a kid like me. I'm pretty disorganized—I sleep late at night, at 3:40 AM to be precise, when only bats and owls keep me company and wake up as late as possible though my dad is really strict and wouldn't let me have my ways, try hard as I'm wont to. Wonder of wonders, I do not brush my teeth, poop twice a week if I'm really lucky, and generally avoid taking a shower—my classmates find me stinking and have the cheek to even tell me so, and I hate them for this. And guys, dare you snigger! What was the last time you saw a lion take a shower or brush his teeth? Get the idea?

My sister's friends are pretty disgusting—I will tell you why in a moment, but dude, aren't those babes hot, red hot! They refuse to even shake hands with me while they have no qualms about riding pillion with my brother on his fancy red motorcycle, just because he's so handsome and beefed up too. I hate them!

I'm thin, do not play any sports, and am quite envious of the beefy types that crowd my grade—the reason I don't go swimming is that you are on show there in your trunks, and what do I boast of? My bones that stick out so shamelessly! And why do girls go for the six-pack types, may I ask? They obviously have nothing else to do than build their bodies. Even the woodcutter I pass on my way to school has muscles and huge ones at that. I don't think they fancy their chances with him!

I think I'm quite brainy—big deal that I don't study. The day I study, I will beat the smartest guy around, I brag to myself and look at the class topper with contempt. Even though my grades are really poor, my father hasn't given up. Somehow, he has the bright idea that his son is a genius, "The day Arjun starts studying, he will beat everyone. The problem is, this child doesn't study at all," he'd tell my mom with pride, finishing off with a sigh.

And then I've a problem with public speaking too—I wonder how people can speak so effortlessly and confidently before large audiences and hate the president of the student union for his bravado—Imagine all the girls swooning over him the moment he is on stage and opens his mouth to talk some crap! Just wait, a day would come when I would vanquish you and the very same girls would sing paeans in my praise, I assure myself, though not with much conviction, I must admit. And then, as if life were not complicated enough already, it is the policy of my school that every kid must be on stage one day and talk, and I dread the very thought that one day I too would need to be on stage and speak.

But the day inevitably dawns, and I am up there, my mouth dry, feet trembling and breath tortured, waiting for my turn. And my fellow students appear to be waiting for the chance to tear me apart, diabolical monsters all! And the teachers are even worse. Everyone is there to judge me and pronounce what a failure I am, I apprehend. But, talk I must, I can't be such a loser, I assure myself, and speak. I am no Mark Antony that day but not a failure either. And can you believe it, the audience claps! I then realize that people are not always judging you, that they're willing to give you a chance and that they even sympathize because they might have had such demons to fight too.

Now what could come of a kid like me? Not much, is it? But wait, when there is darkness, light sometimes finds its way, and the transformation could be magical. You will see in some time whether this metamorphosis does really take place.

It's a wintry morning when you just laze in the bed and find it really tedious to stir. For me, it would be a most hateful task for sure and so it is till I'm jolted out of my sweet dreams by my father's angry shouting, "Arjun, you lazy lump, get up!" My mother adores her obnoxious child and is quick to jump to his defense, "Please do not be angry. The boy was awake till late." "Doing what," my father questions sarcastically. "Oh, he was studying so hard because his school has just started and already the kids are burdened with so many assignments," my mother wouldn't give up. "Okay, and this hard work translates into such poor grades! Anyway, wake him up or he will be late for school again. And if he is late thrice, he is marked absent for a day, and the principal calls either you or me to school, remember?" my father continues, relenting a wee bit. "Yes, yes, I know how embarrassed you were the last time. I promise it won't happen again," my mother so sweetly defends. Dad then leaves, and it's my mom's kind cajoling that gets me out of my bed.

My school is strictly meritocratic—You are a star if you top the school and indeed the country in academics and a burden if you just trudge along, and they would love to get rid of kids like me given the first opportunity because we sully their name, in their considered opinion. I hate them for this and would have run away to something less exacting but for my father – he is just so glued to academics that he would not let me even think of it. Not that I have the temerity to tell him of my bright idea! He would beat me black and blue for sure. Fathers can be such tyrants.

Built ages ago, the school is run by Jesuit missionaries who are largely selfless in providing world-class education to their pupils, and the school consistently ranks among the top ten in the country. The school boasts tennis courts, squash, boxing, basketball, soccer, and an Olympic-size swimming pool. Students are encouraged to be vivacious, outgoing extroverts who can claim their place in the sun in any part of the world. And indeed the alumni are dazzling the world with their brilliance after graduating from some of the finest colleges in the US and the UK.

I find myself a misfit here. My inadequacies, perceived or real I'm not sure at the moment, make me a loner who struggles to be as inconspicuous as possible. I'm the proverbial backbencher who would wish with all his might that the teachers just let him be and instead, direct all their questions to the brilliant lot occupying the front seats. But, there is also the deep-seated feeling that I will beat the class topper by a mile the day I start studying, a blessing from my father who always considered me a genius who just needs to wake up and claim his place in the sun. He has his own parental sixth sense, but factually too, he is not entirely mistaken. As a four-year-old, I had shown great proficiency with numbers, adding up big numbers in an instant. I had a natural flair for English too and as you would see later, I would consider both English and math my fief.

I could never muster the courage to engage in public speaking, but my principal, when I was in the seventh grade, heard me recite a poem that every student was obliged to do and was quite impressed. He declared in the class, "Mark my words. This boy is going to be a great orator someday." Was he being prophetic?

Well, at this point in time, such prophecies seem to be far-fetched. To know why, let me tell you something really sad—I failed my grade nine finals and as per the policy of the school, I have to repeat the year in the same class. It has been a huge setback for the entire family and a severe damage to my self-image because somewhere, in the deepest recesses of my heart, I never considered myself a failure. Maybe my father's belief in my latent ability had touched the core of my heart, and I felt I would come good some day. I'm extremely sensitive too despite all my outer bravado and get easily hurt when someone insults me. And this vulnerability would trouble me much later in life too. But this is my nature and I can do nothing about it. I would now recount a very humiliating experience that I had to bear with utter helplessness.

It was the first day of the new semester, and I was quietly sitting in a corner. I was early and looking rather smart in my school uniform. Soon, the other kids started entering the classroom, and some got curious to find a new face among themselves. One of them walked up to my seat and shook my hand warmly, "Hey, new kid?" "Oh, he is just a repeater. He failed," bellowed a voice, that of the class representative. It really hurt, and I could hardly fight back my tears. Always an introvert, I now found it increasingly difficult to communicate with fellow kids. The fear lurked that some or the other kid would shame me. The teachers seemed terrible too because they neglected me. At least, this is what I felt. They may not have been really unkind but were definitely not perceptive enough to understand that I needed some encouragement to do well.

CHAPTER TWO

I did have my beautiful moments earlier. When I was five years old, my father was posted at Gumla, a scenic town nestled in the hills. I was fond of singing popular songs while pedaling my bike—it's quite another matter that I remembered only a few lines that I kept repeating. But, it was a joyful abandon that marked those fabulous years. I was not very particular about my studies but often impressed my teachers with oral calculations. Many a time it used to happen that I blurted out answers to sums only just written on the blackboard. But when my teachers asked me to show the steps to the solution, I was clueless. My father was ecstatic about his son's brilliance and would often call me a genius.

I was quite courageous too. In our house, there was a bedroom from whose window we could see the local morgue situated at some distance. Dad would challenge us kids, "Now, which one of you is brave enough to sleep in this room alone in the night? One who does, will get chocolates in the morning." And I would be the one to take up the challenge every time, my siblings too scared to even think of that possibility. And my father would kiss my forehead, "My brave son!" Much later in life, when I would be so fearful, I would wonder—Was I the same lionheart who feared nothing at such a tender age? And would cry in frustration.

My grandmother used to recount anecdotes from mythology to which I was attention personified. I loved to hear about Lord Krishna Who performed superhuman feats—when it was pouring in Vrindavan, Krishna lifted an entire mountain on His little finger, and all the inhabitants, including the animals, found refuge under it. When a monstrous snake tried to poison the freshwater lake supplying water to the village, Krishna climbed atop his head in a cosmic dance and vanquished him. I loved his pranks as a naughty toddler, stealing butter and feigning such cute innocence on getting caught that everyone forgave Him.

My father lived in a bungalow with an elaborate inner courtyard that had mango trees. When it was windy during summer, ripe mangoes would fall in the courtyard, and my grandmother would pick them up and offer the most luscious ones to me, her darling. This act of supposed partiality was not liked by my siblings, and they would protest loudly, "Granny, this is not fair. We are your kids too." My grandmother would be at pains to convince them, "Oh no, you all are my babies and equally dear to me. I'm not being partial to Arjun at all." And yet, she would continue to pamper me.

I had four huge dogs, all Alsatians. They simply loved me and would be at my command. When I felt irritated with my siblings or friends, I would order them, "Shoo, catch them," and had a hearty laugh when the kids ran for their lives. Luckily, no one was ever bitten. The dogs loved me a lot. Whenever I returned home after a vacation with my parents, the dogs would crowd around me with a complaining look as if saying, "Why were you away for so long? We were so lost without you." And then, they would put their paws on my shoulders and lick my face. It was so devastating when a few of them were no more—Tiger was injured in the leg by a speeding car and never recovered, Tony caught some infection and couldn't survive. I cried bitterly and was inconsolable, my pain dulling gradually with time and the love of my grandmother.

A few years later, my father was transferred to Patna—a big city bustling with people, polluted, and very hot. I was not at ease at all here, sorely missing the pristine beauty of Gumla. I hated the heat and just wished to be in cool climes once again. I was admitted to one of the finest schools in the city but found its strict discipline and dry academics stifling. I was a free bird who learned best when left to his own ways. Also, the insistence on rote learning, which was the bane of the Indian education system at that time, never could find acceptance from a kid who would rather understand a concept and apply it. Consequently, I performed poorly in the tests except for math. My father was not comfortable with his colleagues and was under a lot of stress. My mother, extremely kind and affectionate, tried to comfort her husband to her level best. But something very tragic was to happen.

One day, my father complained of severe chest pain and had to be rushed to the ICU. My siblings and I were escorted to our maternal grandparents' house by an uncle and learned later that our father had a severe heart attack—he was just forty. It's difficult to say why this happened. I would learn later that, in his younger days, he used to smoke a lot and had a pretty disorganized life before his marriage.

Whatever be the reason, my father was a changed man after that fateful day. A very courageous man at the core, he was more and more worried about the future of his family with four small kids.

One evening, Mom found him really low and couldn't help but question, "What's the matter, you seem so dejected?" "Well, nothing much really, just thinking," Dad tried to evade, not wishing to burden her with any of his fears. "But there's something that's troubling you. You are not the kind who would sit so quietly," Mom persisted. Dad could still have been evasive but wished deeply to share his burden and who would be better suited than his dear wife? "I'm just worried about the future. I've been so ill, on a forced leave for two months now. We are running our house with the help of your father and..." he blurted out in desperation. "But you're getting better now and will soon resume your duty. It's not that we need continuous help from anyone," Mom interrupted. "But I'd such a terrible attack. I'm really worried whether I'll be able to fulfill your needs for all times to come. Will I live long enough for my beautiful kids," Dad said in a choking voice, tears welling in his eyes. "Oh, don't worry, don't panic. You say you've complete faith in Lord Krishna. You claim nothing can really go wrong with you because Lord Krishna protects you always. Is this your faith? What faith is this, that crumbles the moment trouble lurks," Mom questioned. I felt she was really being melodramatic and found it hard to suppress a giggle. Dad, however, seemed to be impressed and cried with relief and renewed vigor, "Oh, so true. If I am worrying, I'm not honoring Krishna. I would rather Him take care of everything than worry about anything." I wondered whether Krishna really takes care of everything.

The same night I was playing with my brothers, throwing a hard ball and catching it. By mistake, my throw hit my father on the head. I was terrified, wondering if I had hurt my father grievously. That night, for the first time, I prayed to Lord Krishna, "God, please, please save my father. I can't lose him."

After a while, my father recovered and resumed his duty. But hardly had the family recovered that my grandmother died. She had fractured her hip and was confined to her bed. She was a brave lady and tried her level best to regain her health, but that was not to be. I was very sad because I was really attached to her.

Time is a great healer, and soon I was playful again. Then, my father was transferred to Ranchi at a higher position. Ranchi was pleasantly cool, and I loved the crisp breeze. Life was a party because my father was in a very high position. We were invited to theatres to watch the latest films; restaurant owners seemed to fall over themselves to serve the family of the top bureaucrat; and to top it all, the best schools vied to admit us kids. My brothers and I used to go to tutorials in the evening but hardly studied. Instead, we loved to eat ice cream at the local supermarket.

The school I attended was full of brilliant students, and I again felt quite out of place. Also, the students were told strictly to converse in English only during their school hours. I could hardly do so as I was not at all fluent in spoken English, even though I could write well. I, however, decided one day that enough was enough, and I must converse in English. So, I took my younger brother along on a mission to procure a monthly bus pass for my sister after speaking to the concerned clerk in English. What followed was an ordeal, and the clerk was incredulous to find some kid struggling with English at such an elite school. But I could convey what I desired, and the clerk issued the pass, and with this small accomplishment, I took a big step in life—If you truly desire and give it a good try, you can achieve your goal. Of course, this big lesson had to wait to be fully realized by this not-so-serious kid.

We kids were so busy enjoying and the school we attended had such high standards that all of us just scraped through our finals. Our parents were extremely embarrassed but felt they too were partly responsible for the poor grades. Dad was extremely busy with his office and had poor health too. Mom was not keeping well and felt really low though there was apparently no reason to feel gloomy. But, despite all the worldly gains if your spouse is not keeping well and has had such a terrible ailment, any woman, whatever be her composure, would be affected and probably due to this reason, she felt so forlorn.

Now let me tell you about my older brother, Yudi, a pretty complicated guy. He is just two years older and hence, felt quite neglected when I was born. As happens in all families, people get quite enamored by the newborn and even though they really care for the older kid, attention does get divided. My older brother was so annoyed that he threw a toy car at me when I was just a couple of months old. My father was angry and really scolded him to the effect that the toddler chose to go to his maternal grandmother's house and stay there. My father thought it was just a passing phase and didn't bother. This was a serious mistake as the kid felt he was unwelcome in his parents' house. Later, he went to Delhi with his grandparents, the father still persisting in his folly. This time he felt the kid would get a better education there. The kid continued feeling neglected, and it was quite heart-wrenching to find him carrying his cricket gear every time he came home during vacations, resolving that he would live with his parents. My father was posted at Gumla and correctly felt that the child would get a much better education in Delhi. But the kid was truly alienated from his family and deeply hurt, unknown to his father all his life but revealed to his mother much later by his wife in whom he sought solace. Everyone felt the pain but what had been terribly wronged, though very unknowingly, could never be completely healed.

I was very attached to my brother and considered him my savior whenever I was bullied. I was not really strong and got scared easily. But then I secretly told myself, "You wretches, just wait. Let my brother come and he will punch you hard." But I was also worried when I learned that one of the bullies had really strong hands, "What if he really hurts Yudi! I must not endanger his life." And I would tremble with fear.

It's however really sad that my brother was always unaware of my affection.

Ranchi days were over when my father was again transferred. Dad respected his dignity and when a powerful politician insulted him because he refused to connive in his corrupt deeds, he gave him a mouthful. As a result, he was transferred before the completion of his tenure. On the flight back to Patna, something interesting happened—there was mid-air turbulence and everyone was scared but not my father who reasoned that there was no need to fear because if the plane crashed, you straightaway go to meet your Maker. "It's scarier on a train or a car because you risk physical injury," he continued nonchalantly. Strange logic but something that went straight to my heart, and I would never dread a flight even when I grew up, whatever be the turbulence.

CHAPTER THREE

Coming back to where we left off, I found it an ordeal to go back to the same grade and endure all the insults I was subjected to by some of the classmates—You would find it hard to believe how cruel some kids can be at even such a tender age. I continued to perform poorly and that made the principal very angry. One day, he summoned my father and told him very clearly that a student with such poor grades was just not fit for such an elite school and that he should consider withdrawing me and putting me in some other school where the academic standards were not so high. When my father came out of the principal's office, his eyes were brimming with tears, and I can never forget his pain. But he didn't scold me at all. Instead, he took me to my favorite restaurant and ordered my favorite food. When I was at ease and eating, my father spoke, "Son, what happened today was most unfortunate. Your principal was so annoyed that he straightaway asked me to admit you to some other school. He feels you are not good enough for his school. What do you think?" I stopped eating and was speechless. Dad noticed my discomfiture and told me very calmly, "Son, be at ease. I am neither blaming you nor scolding you. I'm just offering you a choice—do you want to quit the school and seek solace in mediocrity, or will you determine to turn over a new leaf and prove to the world what you are made of? To me, you are a genius who just needs to focus." I was overwhelmed. Tears welling in my eyes, I promised with grim resolve, "Dad, I will never let you down again. I would prove to the world that I'm next to none." Blessing me, my father's eyes shone with pride. No doubts, no skepticism.

My father advised me to pray to Lord Hanuman. Lord Hanuman is believed to cut out all negativity from one's life and also, to bless the devotee with health, strength, and wisdom. I surely needed all of them the way my life was in a shambles then. I started praying fervently, and lo, it was magic! I was able to concentrate and, blessed with a sharp brain, made rapid progress. It seemed some higher force was pushing me to persevere and do better and better. I was still sleeping late but not wasting my time in idle thoughts—I was studying hard and still getting up in time for school. After just a few months of diligence, I was among the top ten in the class. Jealous classmates tried to find fault, saying I was doing so well because I was a repeater. Didn't I know the syllabus already? Didn't I fail just a few months ago? "He is just mediocre," they would say dismissively and with loads of scorn. I was extremely sensitive and got hurt easily, but some extraordinary power was propelling me and would not let me wallow in self-pity, and I just couldn't stop studying. A time came when my father had to compel me to take a break and go play.

It seemed I was set for a great life but troubles dogged me again. It was most devastating when my father was suspended from service on some trumped-up charges. His fault—he couldn't bow down and participate in the wrongdoings of corrupt seniors. The family was in a state of shock because not only was there a loss of reputation but also a financial crisis—my father was to be paid only half his salary till he was exonerated. Mom was forced to seek help from her father who did all he could. But he was already retired and ill, and Dad was not going to pester him at all. Desperately trying to salvage the situation, he hit upon the idea of setting up a business. Dogged by ill health, nevertheless, he climbed five floors when required to negotiate a deal. Here was a man made of some tough material, the kind you come across not often in life. God responded, and he was able to secure some agencies from steel tube manufacturers, earning a percentage as commission. But this business required constant travelling throughout the state, and he was forced to rope in his eldest son to do the legwork as his health was so fragile—he had a terrible heart condition, remember? He was very protective of me, however, because he felt I shouldn't divert my attention from studies and didn't let me engage in business at all. This decision was probably not right.

CHAPTER FOUR

It's not easy to earn from business, and Dad was forced to seek loans from different banks. Most of them were not interested, but a few obliged. Loan seekers were not particularly respected in the society we lived in. People felt that the money borrowed was used to meet household expenses too besides funding a struggling business. Once my father took the family out for an ice cream treat to one of the posh shopping complexes. We just wanted to have a good time after seemingly perpetual hardships. But as luck would have it, the manager of the bank that had lent a substantial loan to the family happened by. Full of sarcasm, he called out to Dad, "Oh, you are here. I didn't imagine you would visit such expensive places." My father's face lost all color in embarrassment, and the family was shamed to the core. I will never forget how pitiable my father looked when he tried to explain his level best that he was not splurging bank money, "Uh, I never wanted to come, but these kids insisted so much. I'm so busy trying to get some orders. And we had some profits of late. I'm not using any of the bank money to indulge these kids, you know." I seethed with suppressed anger—What right has this guy to publicly insult my father? Is this money his paternal property? He is just a paid employee who's getting his bank a substantial amount as interest for the loan disbursed.

Later, when I grew up, I would dread the very thought of taking a loan even when phone banking officers enticed me with hundreds of offers promising easy loans.

I was excelling at academics all along, and the teachers were surprised. The same principal, who had once told my father to withdraw me from his fancy school, was forced to exclaim, "How is this kid transformed like this! It seems a miracle has taken place." But the financial situation was going from bad to worse. I remember very vividly the hard times when people only made fun of my father, and none helped except for my maternal grandfather for whom his daughter was most precious. Mom hated the very idea of taking money from her old father but had no choice. At school, one of the devilish classmates called my father a thief, and I could do nothing. I felt so terrible, so helpless. Some of my friends were innocuous, but even they could hurt, so deplorable was the financial situation. One of them casually remarked, "We are all so well-to-do that we can afford anything. Just imagine, in whose house is the table not laid out with the choicest of fruits at lunch or dinner?" Everyone nodded in agreement, and I was compelled to do the same out of embarrassment, and I hated myself for lying. It had been ages since the family had fruits.

I often yearned for the fine fabric that went into making my classmates' uniforms as my uniform was made of ordinary cotton. My father's car was due for repairs, but there was no money. Once, when I was sitting in the front seat, I noticed a gaping hole in the floorboard through which hot air was hitting my foot and felt very sad.

When the final results were out, I was in for some very pleasant surprise. I had topped the grade and was filled with pride. Now in grade ten, I was still studying very hard, forsaking any kind of pleasure. My maternal grandfather was very proud of me but also critical whenever I didn't get a perfect score. I used to be very annoyed, complaining to my grandfather, "But I topped the class!" My grandfather was a perfectionist and would accept nothing below a perfect score, something that made my father laugh heartily as he had known his father-in-law's quirkiness for so many years.

The family suffered another setback when my grandfather died of a paralytic stroke. Now, the big question was, "Who will help when the going is so tough?"

Academically, I was going from strength to strength, clearing my grade ten finals with flying colors, featuring among the top twenty in the state. Because of my spiritual connection with Lord Hanuman, I was supremely confident of myself and actually declared that I was going to top just after finishing my finals. I had my entire life planned out too—at this age, I would take the Indian Administrative Service (IAS) exam, top it and would be on my way to becoming a top bureaucrat; then, at this point in time, I would become a top-notch writer because that had been my ambition right from my childhood; and so on. Getting into the IAS was my dream because I'd seen the trappings of power that came along with such an elite service, having seen my father as a senior bureaucrat. My father marveled at my confidence and used to ask in amusement, "How are you so cocksure of everything?" My English teacher would say, with mild sarcasm, “When you talk, you will not talk of anyone less than Shakespeare.” My teachers just loved me.

I launched into bodybuilding too and, genetically blessed with a strong body, built a fantastic physique. I was so muscular that my proud father banned my body-fit tees, fearing his son might fall sick because of envious eyes.

I got into debating and dramatics with a vengeance, winning several awards for stellar performances. All of a sudden, I was offered the central role of Santa Claus in a fab play. Instinctive to the core, I was just brilliant. I was full of ideas, too. In the original play, Santa came on a sleigh pulled by reindeer, but I had some other ideas, suggesting to the director, “Sir, I would rather ride my motorcycle through the auditorium to the stage.” Now, my bike was a slim one, not at all like the humongous monsters you come across in Hollywood flicks. The director was aghast, “How is it possible! The auditorium will be pitch dark, packed with invitees, and you will be traversing the aisle. The audience consists mostly of students, and just imagine, some naughty kid puts his foot out just when the bike is crossing that patch! The whole show will end in a fiasco.” To add to all this complexity, I was supposed to balance a globe, perched precariously between the handlebars. But I persisted and did it in style. The moment I approached the stage, I turned on the headlights of my bike and, taking the cue, the stage lights were switched on. There were so many catcalls from girls that I felt truly like a star. Some parents thought I was a professional actor and were surprised to know that I was still a student.

The next morning, the entertainment section of the leading daily had my picture prominently displayed, flanked by my leading ladies. The whole family was proud, and I was thrilled to find that look of admiration in my father's eyes.

Everything seemed just perfect, a beautiful life seemed to beckon, and I was ecstatic. But there were dark clouds lurking on the horizon, and a storm threatened to break loose.

CHAPTER FIVE

Dad lost his case at the sessions court but was lucky to escape imprisonment, securing bail. He filed an appeal in the high court and all this cost money that was so hard to come by. Lawyers were so expensive, and there were frequent trips to Delhi where the suit was going on. At this juncture, he was forced to ask his eldest son to actively participate in business. He however still desisted from involving me, fearing my attention would wander. As time progressed and business needed more hands to cope with the pressure, even my younger brother, Karan, joined in. Money started flowing, but my father was still too frail to run around. As my brothers were active participants, questions began to be raised—Why is Arjun not participating? Why has he been let off while others slog?

My brothers were full of scorn, "Oh! He's good for nothing, just a parasite, a burden!" Once, when a cousin learned that my father preferred my brothers, which was not really true, he sarcastically remarked, "Why not? Aren't they the earning ones? Who cares for losers like Arjun who are nothing but parasites!"

My aunts would be incredulous, "Oh, you don't do business, only study!"

I was, and I am, extremely sensitive and very hurt by these barbs. I would wonder—Isn't a kid supposed to study? What sin am I committing if I love to study? But I failed to understand that the circumstances were not normal. My father was not running around and even though it was his guidance, my brothers felt they were running the show because, after all, they were doing the legwork. Dad didn't foresee the implications for my life. It would have been prudent to induct me into the business, too. I was such a good student that I would have excelled with even a few hours of study that I would have easily managed at night.

It was at this time that I started getting distracted from my studies. I felt people were blaming me only because I was so engrossed in my books. It was a cardinal mistake because my identity stemmed from academic brilliance; it was what I had always yearned for even when my grades were terrible. What I failed to realize was that my failures in the past stemmed from distraction and not because I was intellectually mediocre and hence, a repeat of the same would spawn the same terrible past. I started skipping college too because my younger brother was too busy to attend at times, and even close friends would question, "Oh, your brother is away on business, but he lets you attend. He's so selfless." My younger brother and I were in the same class because he was only a year younger, and I repeated a year in school.

Something even more terrible was happening. I was getting confused with religion. I worshipped Lord Hanuman but then felt compelled to pray to other deities too—What if they became angry? And then I trembled with the thought. It was a ruminating thought that went on and on, weakening me terribly from within. From a deeply spiritual connection, my devotion deteriorated into ritualism. Now, prayers were not my bulwark against all storms; they rather suffocated me. Lord Hanuman, however, was warning me not to commit hara-kiri, and I was often reminded of a story in which a mouse morphed into a really powerful being with divine grace but became a mouse again when he lost that grace. Yet, I didn't listen and continued on my suicidal path, sinking deeper into the morass. And with the spiritual disconnect, dissipated my inner strength, and I was reduced to despondency and despair.

Thus, I was thrown into a vicious whirlpool—my circumstances were pathetic, but I might have emerged victorious with my deep faith, but this faith vanished, the vacuum filled with dread that something would go wrong if I didn't propitiate a myriad of deities. In other words, my very power became my arch-enemy.

My grades began to suffer, and Dad was incredulous – Why doesn't he study after all? What the hell is he up to when he is doing so well? I didn't share my inner chaos with my father though I did tell him that I wanted to meet a psychiatrist. My father couldn't understand why and was summarily dismissive, "There's nothing wrong with you. You are just disturbed. Steer clear of unnecessary thoughts and, for God's sake, just study." But there was something terribly wrong—I was so distressed that I was losing interest in everything I loved and had earned so painstakingly. Gone was my obsession with bodybuilding, debating, and dramatics, and it's just beyond comprehension how even my parents couldn't figure out my tragedy.

CHAPTER SIX

I was slowly losing my identity. Extremely instinctive, I was free like a bird that flies without limits wherever it wishes, without a care in the world. This was my true identity and this way, I'd always been in sync with myself and hence, at ease. During my childhood, I would break into a dance, sing a song even though I would remember just a few lines, bicycle with gay abandon, and so on. But now, I sought to conform, to please, lest my brothers become offensive and wound my very core, and this was a terrible mistake. Much later in life, I would do the same and suffer terribly until I realized that this was not really me and that I should do something about it. But much damage would have been done by then. And yet, I would rebound with great power and once in sync with myself, my life would change dramatically.

Once, during my troubled times, we all were watching a movie, and one of the lead actors called another, who was jobless, a parasite. I quaked with apprehension that my brothers would call me the same, and this exactly happened. My elder brother casually said, "Hey, aren't you a parasite too? You do nothing." And I cried and cried that night, mumbling uncontrollably, "I'm not a parasite, I'm not a parasite," tortured tears streaming down my face.

Losing one's identity is always tragic because your instinct is the inner voice, the inner compass, that guides you through several twists and turns life is inextricably heir to. When you follow your instinct, you are in sync with the divine will that exactly knows what's optimal for you and the decisions that you make invariably serve your greatest good. Even mundane chores are best performed when you're guided by instinct. While walking, your instinct tells you that you have walked enough for the day; while lifting weights, it's again your instinct that tells you when to stop; and when you are driving your car, it's again instinct that tells you whether there is enough room to manoeuvre on a busy crossroads. Of late, I have been following my instinct when I am in the washroom, and everything has been so smooth, no constipated bowel movements at all!

An actor performs best when he is swayed by emotions. So does an artist, a writer, a singer. I truly believe that if you're pursuing any art, just float on your instinct so that conscious reasoning, confused by societal expectations, does not hinder this life force. If you've the divinely blessed superstar quotient, it will shine through. For that matter, whatever be your ability, if you afford free play to your instinct, you'll operate at your level best.

It's extremely important to stay calm when you want your instinct to function properly because agitation disturbs your inner rhythm. You should be fearless, too, because fear has the terrible power to confuse and freeze the best minds. So just follow these steps: stay calm, do not fear, and let your instinct kick in. And it would be magic!

Alas! I was not following my instinct during my troubled times even though Lord Hanuman had been warning me all through, and I would go through hell before finding bliss. But more of that later.

Even when the clouds are dark, they do have a silver lining at times. So while I was absolutely distracted from studies, I found solace elsewhere. One morning, I just walked up to my father and declared, “Dad, I feel, I too should be a part of your business. Tell me what I should start with.” “But why, son? I told you, you just study. I'm there to take care of business, and your brothers are so cooperative too. I would rather you go to Oxford or Cambridge. That's where you belong. Business is not your cup of tea, for sure. You're too much of an idealist to succeed in this dog-eat-dog world,” my father reasoned. “But Dad, my brothers are a part of the same, and I don't want to be a passive observer. I will come good, you will see,” I insisted. “Okay, if you're so adamant,” Dad agreed reluctantly. He still didn't know how miserable I was, and I was very sure this agony would not stretch any more, and thus, I plunged into business with a vengeance. Soon, my father entrusted me with negotiations with foreigners as the family now was importing medical equipment for sale in big hospitals. Dapper in my expensive suits, I just floored foreign delegates who marveled at my command of English and business savvy. My brothers were happy because now everyone was working. Their only grievance had been: why should one of them enjoy the fruits of their labor while not contributing to business at all? They were, after all, very young too and did not understand how damaging their behavior was to their brother's psyche. My elder brother was so impressed by my business acumen that he felt it was unnecessary to accompany me to business meetings that my father was insisting upon, feeling I was too raw. "You are so good that I'm just a silent observer," gushed he, and I was ecstatic because I always craved recognition.

CHAPTER SEVEN

Business was doing well, and now was the time to celebrate. The three of us brothers embarked on a pleasure-cum-shopping trip to Kathmandu, a big shopping list in tow because Dad wanted so many things from abroad. He just loved fine, imported stuff that was so hard to get in India at that time. The government had a closed-doors policy, forcing the commoner to make do with low-quality stuff produced within the country while the rich and the powerful splurged on imported goods shamelessly. Law then, at times, was very lopsided, which an Indian today would find hard to comprehend as we get all the top brands in the world freely. And my father loved those expensive watches and perfumes and pens and whatnot—you name it. We bought and bought, dined at five-star hotels and generally had a great time. I was working out again and had built a fab physique that men envy and women desire. My elder brother would always tell me to strike up a conversation with beautiful girls because he was so sure, "No one can resist you. You're just too handsome." And then, sheepishly, "And why don't you introduce me to some of them," and I would feel so happy. I love adulation and nothing makes me happier than someone praising me so openly. Man, I was on a roll!

And then I met Jane. She was an Australian, and we came across in a casino where she had come with a friend. She couldn't take her eyes off me, and I too liked her tall, statuesque body. And then she said, "Hi, you come here often?" I was waiting for this and spoke in my baritone, "Not really. I'm an Indian and just visiting. And where are you from?" "Australia," she said and then we hit it upon really well. My brothers smiled mischievously, but I didn't bother. Then, it was time for her to leave, but she left with an invitation, "There's this fancy disc, Thamil. Why don't you drop in tomorrow night? We will have a great time." I was excited—This babe sure is interested. Man, why don't you just do something about it! And I was all set for the party the next night.

It so happened that I found no cabs that night, and the only alternative was to catch a bus. The bus kept me waiting and then, this guy materialized from nowhere and started talking, "Hey, you Indian?" "Yeah," I said, not sure what he wanted. I wished not to talk but he persisted, and I don't know why I started talking myself. He then asked me, "Where are you going so late in the night?" I should have said, "Get lost, that's none of your business." But I told him that I had been invited by this chick, and I was just searching for conveyance. He was aghast, "What are you talking! These foreigners have all kinds of diseases. Who knows you contract one, you'll find no cure." I'm still unsure why I believed that stranger but was sufficiently spooked to scurry back to my hotel and gone was my chance to have that first hot night. Yeah, I was a virgin then!

Now, I must tell you about my libido. Strongly driven by sex, I was an alpha male, wild like the storm that rages unchained, unbound, limitless. My mates would be voluptuous women with an hourglass figure, a beautiful face, and a spotless complexion. It's another matter that I got none and so much for sweet dreams! My cousins wondered whom I would fall in love with at all, as my big body—six feet tall, rippling with muscles—with a handsome face and a voice to die for, could enamor anyone, and it happened quite a few times. When I was doing theatre, girls would try to be really pally, but I would evade them, maybe because they were not my type or because I didn't want commitment. My classmates would try to get close too, but Patna had a huge problem at that time. Invariably, there would be a rogue around, warning me, "Bro, that's my girl. Steer clear of her or else..." It's another matter that the girl in question would not even be aware that this speck of dirt even existed. But these guys were serious trouble, protected by local politicians, and their threats were not to be taken lightly.

One evening, I was visiting the local club my father was a member of. And then I saw Vini. Man, was she pretty—pinkish, extremely well-endowed, and what a face! I was besotted. I was quick to approach, "Hey, new to the club? I'm Arjun." I knew none could resist me, and I was right. She replied warmly, "Not really. My father is a member." Encouraged, I continued, "But never saw you here?" "Well, that's because I'm studying in Delhi. I'm here on a vacation. And I'm Vini. Good to meet you." We kept talking for some more time, and I felt this was my chance. Finally, I got someone I desired. When I asked for her number, she obliged. And I was on cloud nine. We then talked on the phone often, but she never agreed to come on a date, and this disturbed me. Then, one fine day, a friend told me she'd already left for Delhi. I was incredulous, "It's impossible! We talk every day." "Someone is taking you for a ride. Check it out for yourself," my friend advised. And that night, I bluntly asked the girl, "Who the hell are you? Vini apparently has left for Delhi already." "Well, I'm her mother, and this phone she uses only in Patna," she answered. "But why should you impersonate your daughter? I felt I was talking to her all along," I questioned angrily. "That's because I needed to know how well you all knew each other," she replied shamelessly. I disconnected immediately, thinking she must be one of the frustrated aunties my friends often talked about while discussing their escapades with older women. Thus ended my first really serious adventure with a babe I liked so much. And wonder of wonders, we never met again.

CHAPTER EIGHT

Something interesting happened while I was holidaying in Darjeeling, a beautiful place up in the hills where clouds waft below your feet. I was with my younger brother and a cousin, Rob, and so charming did we appear that many other tourists called us the three musketeers. One evening, we spotted two beautiful teenagers at a coffee shop. As usual, I was entrusted with the task of chatting them up, and I would never say I wouldn't. I entered the lounge in style, pulled a chair near theirs and sat down. After ordering coffee, I casually asked, "Hey, you Brits?" The girls looked at each other with surprise and then replied, "Well, we are. But how did you figure that out!" I said earlier that no chick could resist a hunk like me and see how my charm was working. I smiled and let out the secret, "Intuition." The girls were pleasantly skeptical, "Oh, it's so!" and then introduced themselves, "Hey, I'm Liza and she's Kate." "This is Arjun and glad to meet you," I said with a firm handshake, holding that lovely hand just a bit longer. Then, an invite escaped my lips, "Why don't we meet for dinner? It's so pleasant today." The girls looked at each other and then smiled, "Oh, why not. But where?" "Well, there's a nice joint down the road, Broadway. The food is supposed to be great. There. Nine o'clock tonight. I will wait for you." "Okay," the chicks said and finishing coffee, we went out together. But the story is not over yet. Outside, at some distance, my brother and my cousin were waiting, smoking. I tried to drop a hint that they should come and join us and not wait at a distance, but they didn't understand and kept watching. The girls noticed, however, and must have felt there was something fishy. Anyways, we parted with warm handshakes, and I felt the night was going to be memorable.

In the night, I was all set for my date and so was my brother who literally hounded me in his quest to join the fun, "How will you handle two chicks? Let me have one and you've the other one. Whoever you like you take, I'm fine with any of them." I was naughty, "You think I can't handle them both! Bro, just wait and watch." My brother would not give up, "Please, I'm your kid brother." And I agreed, "Ok, hop in."

My cousin was literally smothering everyone with dollops of perfume, and I was aghast, "Dude, why are you so charged up! There are only two babes, one for me and one for Karan." But my cousin insisted that he, at least, could come for dinner, and I had no choice. We were at Broadway at nine o'clock sharp, but the girls were nowhere to be seen, and we kept waiting. It was an hour, but the girls didn't turn up. I then figured out that the two, being foreigners, must have got scared when my brother and cousin didn't join in but kept staring and smoking from a distance. "Who knows, these guys might be goons," they might have thought. And I was furious—What a waste! I shouldn't have taken note of these guys or exited the lounge alone. Another opportunity lost and I stayed a virgin. Well, that's what I thought. But, just maybe those babes were coming for dinner only and had no plans for some hot action thereafter. I wouldn't feel like that at that time as I was so young and deluded like many my age.

CHAPTER NINE

I was seemingly happy but not so really. I was deeply connected to God and derived all my strength from the Infinite Source. But my confusion with myriad forms persisted. Sometimes, out of utter despair, I felt like worshipping Krishna alone and none else. Was it a conspiracy by Lord Hanuman to guide me to the Supreme Lord because what more could He have done for his favorite devotee! This was the ultimate in affection. Krishna is God Himself and reaching Him is the biggest goal anyone can dream of.

I was so troubled that I stopped praying. God was not oblivious to my travails though and indicated that He is the One Infinite Source, different forms just reflections of that Light. I'd this moment of epiphany in a vision that is too personal to be discussed in detail. And I was wide awake when I saw that moment of ultimate truth. I was at peace for some time, but fear confused me again.

Fear has that strange power because it's always so vague. People start feeling that if they do a particular thing some disaster will ensue. But what disaster, may I ask? Have you gone ahead and checked it out for yourself that yes, there are some hidden demons out there? Actually, it never has any substance and if you call its bluff, it will cringe away. Can you imagine that it takes just one bold step to check out the truth for yourself and then you're free, and how sweet is that freedom! Else, fear will limit you till you're strangled, gasping for that last breath because fear is so cruel it will not let you even breathe for a moment. So do exactly what fear asks you not to do and see how it cowers away. Unfortunately, I didn't know this at that time and suffered terribly.

I feared that my family would be destroyed if I didn't worship a certain number of deities. And the number of deities kept growing because there are so many forms and so was the perceived disaster that included now not only my immediate family but also relatives beyond. Fear was paralyzing me, and I was just too confused to sit and analyze even for a few moments. In hindsight, I could have just calmed down and questioned the bluff—Okay, fear is threatening me with a particular disaster. Let's see if it comes true. When things did not happen the way fear predicted they would, I would be emboldened. Then another challenge and yet another, victory all along, and finally, freedom from fear.

I was so troubled that I went ahead and met a psychiatrist without telling my father. The psychiatrist listened to me carefully and then counseled, "Keep off religion for some time. If you are compelled to worship, nonetheless, tell yourself calmly—Okay, I'll do it after some time. This way, you might escape ruminating, repetitive thoughts too."

Heeding his advice, I stopped praying and generally kept

away from any ritual as well. I was able to study now for the grueling IAS exam that the best brains in the country study hard to clear—I'd already graduated from college with not-so-exciting grades, troubled as I was by poor concentration—and even went undisturbed for a few months.

But mine was a deep spiritual connection, the source from which all my strength flowed. The apparent calm was deceptive because I was not at peace with God and hence, not at ease whenever I had a moment of solitude. The solution was not to escape but to face the issue squarely and settle it there and then. NOW is the time you act and act you must, because passivity will never resolve the conflict. The moment I sat down to study, conflicting thoughts troubled my mind. I desperately wanted to study because I desired so earnestly to get into the IAS, but then fear would distract me with all its might, inexorably pulling me into opposing directions, my attention going to the dogs. It was like pressing down the accelerator hard and applying the brakes at the same time. I was not listening to my instinct that was desperately telling me to do one thing at a time—While studying I should study alone; when praying, I should pray alone; when doing business, I should do business alone.

I had read a short story by Leo Tolstoy that grounded everyone into the present so firmly, and only someone crazy enough to self-destruct would ignore those condensed drops of wisdom—an expression so beautifully used by my dear father in one of his write-ups that inspired me so much—precisely what I was doing at that time. And I was ruminating all the time about my fears that made it so hard for me to do something about it. I have figured out that fear alone may not have the power to paralyze. But the moment you allow it to force its way through your every living moment, it becomes terror, debilitating your critical faculties, and then, it's extremely difficult to get out of that vicious circle, something I would endure again and again, making my life absolutely hellish.

So, the moment fear strikes, tackle it there and then. If you cannot, you're in for trouble but at least do not let it possess every aspect of your life, or this would snowball into terror, viciously choking your life.

Surprisingly, I never had any trouble clinching a business deal. Maybe business is all about doing and not ruminating. Maybe it required total immersion, unlike studies that demanded I sit alone and concentrate. Maybe it was my chance to prove myself, something I was so desperately seeking to win approval from my family and relatives. Whatever be it, I was totally at peace while doing business, forgetting all my troubles. And then luck offered me a chance—Would I take it?

CHAPTER TEN

It was the dawn of a new year, and I was feverishly pacing up and down my bedroom. My instinct was telling me to trust Lord Hanuman, surrender everything to Him and just study. But fear was forcing me to immediately go to Benares to perform some rituals that had been promised when business prospered. A calm mind would deliberate—What's the hurry? Your IAS exam, which you desperately want to ace, is around the corner, and it requires you to clear a written examination and that needs loads of concentration. Study hard for now, take your exam and then go wherever you wish to. Benares is not running away. This is a much more pressing issue.

But I didn't listen to my inner voice and bowed down to fear that not only unsettled me thoroughly but also resulted in my failure to clear the coveted exam and that depressed me a lot. This was my first brush with the real world when my father was not able to bequeath his position to me, and I failed so miserably. This was the first time my dream died. Had I just listened to my instinct, I would have been spared much pain and a rejuvenated faith would have resurrected me into someone amazing. There was nothing wrong with me except for my baseless fears, remember? I just needed some support to assert myself and for me, God was the ultimate refuge. Had I just surrendered everything to Lord Hanuman, firmly ensconced in that mindset, entertaining no negative thought even for a moment—it's vitally important that when you surrender to the divine, you should not give in to negative thoughts at all because they have this uncanny ability to pull you out of that bliss, and you will have to struggle extremely hard to clear the confusion and get back into that heaven again—life would have been so magical for me. At all crucial junctures, I allowed fear to fiendishly sabotage my prospects rather than taking refuge in the bliss that Lord Hanuman's grace creates. And when there would be a matter of life and death, myself surrendering everything to Lord Hanuman, a very precious life would be saved. Just imagine, what a hellish journey through life I would have been spared if I had just followed my instinct and left everything to Lord Hanuman. I am sure I would have been telling you a different story, one of magical bliss rather than one of excruciating pain and brutal suffering. How I wish that I never had that "if" in my life, that I had made the right choice at the right time!

It's a strange thing with determination—once you resolve upon a course of action and proceed thereon, brooking no resistance, you grow stronger by the day and the goal you're set upon seems so easy to reach. But the moment you let doubt creep in, your resolve dissolves, and you're back to square one, saddled this time with the burden of failed determination. Weakness replaces firmness, and you're lost in self-doubt and pity, exactly the lot I chose for myself. And Dad just wondered helplessly—What would come of this kid, he just doesn't study! I had such big dreams for him.

The business was suffering too because many multinational corporations making top-quality medical equipment had opened their offices in Patna. They had the advantage of offering world-class after-sales service that my father's small outfit could not afford.

CHAPTER ELEVEN

I was in for the greatest shock of my life. My father—my mentor, my inspiration, my hero—was no more. His passing away was so surreal—I had a nightmare that I had just reached home, alighting from my motorcycle when I saw my brothers carrying dad out, everyone crying. The veranda was awash with lights. I got up in a shock, sweating, "God, this cannot be true. This just can't happen. Please do something, please," my eyes brimming with tears, my heart pounding.

When everyone was lost in sorrow and quite clueless about how life would unfold, my mother was the epitome of strength. She knew her family had suffered a terrible loss, and someone needed to hold it together so that the wounds healed with time. When I cried and cried, my mother would comfort me, "You're your dad's dear child. You can't torment yourself like this. How sad your father would be to see you like this? Take charge of yourself, son. That would make your father happy." And then my younger brother cautioned, "Dad is already gone. If you continue like this, something might happen to Mom. And what will we do then?" And I was jolted back into reality—I can't lose my mom for sure; I must control myself. I found much-needed solace in her lap, and life slowly limped back to normalcy.

My father's death ended my religious turmoil about myriad forms, and I began praying to Lord Hanuman again. Why should this happen? Maybe I needed some solid support now because I was so dependent on my father. I loved my mother but was not so secure with her as with my father—emotions have this crazy thing that's beyond reason—and hence, traveled yonder in my quest for emotional stability, and my heart said, "Lord Hanuman is your anchor." It is really sad that I couldn't decide earlier because then my father would have left in peace, not fretting about my future. But my faith was not absolute the way it had been when I was blessed with the magical transformation I mentioned earlier, and this was not going to suffice when I would face the toughest challenges in life, as I would learn again and again, much to my dismay.

Events moved faster from now on. My sister got married and then my elder brother too. The entry of my brother's wife made it more urgent that I earn from business. I feared I might again be labeled good-for-nothing. Money was hard to come by, and I was quite pessimistic about the future of business. Maybe I was not cut out for business despite all my acumen, and my father was right that I must seek my future in academia. I had this nagging doubt—business has no future, and I don't want to get stuck once it fails. I must try something else and now. This is the only time I have. Alas, this never struck me when I had everything on a platter and my father was around. I just had to study and get into the IAS or build my future as an academic at a fantastic university of my choice—Harvard, Oxford, or Cambridge. I was never in doubt about my success in any of these ventures, so good was I academically. Desperately seeking an option, a wild idea struck my imagination—Why not be a movie star? After all, I'd been so good at acting.

When I told my elder brother about this idea, he was aghast, "Are you crazy! Do you know how hard it's to be a movie star? The movie industry is a bad, bad world where only people with money or influence succeed. You're an escapist who wants to run the moment he finds the going tough, and success always eludes such weaklings. This is the reason you cracked up before the IAS exam." Harsh words but maybe true. My mother, however, was calm and even felt I would succeed. And why not—her kid was six feet tall, dark, handsome, with a fantastic physique, rippling with muscles, and a voice to die for.

I was suddenly full of doubt—Is this the right decision? Papa always said, "Son, never forsake something definite for something uncertain. That's a cardinal mistake." I definitely could do business that earned me respect after so much humiliation that I had to undergo. What really lies beyond? Would it bring success or would it mean more insults that would wound my very soul?

There were practical difficulties too. The film industry was located in Mumbai, and I would need to relocate there. Mumbai was an expensive city, property prices shooting through the roof, and our business was not doing well. So, how would I finance my stay there?

A cousin from the megalopolis came up with a solution, "You could get admitted to Mumbai University and then, get a room in the dorm. This would solve the problem of pricey accommodation, and you could then pursue acting with ease. Lectures get over by the afternoon and then you would be free."

Accordingly, I went ahead to secure admission to the Department of English for a master's degree and then left Patna with great hope. My sister's husband was related to a big film star and, heeding my request, she procured a letter from him, arranging a meeting with the star who might be of some help, I hoped. She, however, was scared to tell her husband about my dreams because he despised film folks. She lied to him brazenly, "Arjun is going to Mumbai for some work and would like to watch some film shoots over there. Maybe you could ask your cousin to arrange for a pass. And he could meet him as well, as he's such a great fan of his." So, my journey began with doubts, lies, fears, and some hope. I boasted, "I'm going by the train but will return by air because producers will queue up to sign me up the moment I step into their offices." And my younger brother believed that.

CHAPTER TWELVE

Mumbai is huge, way different from Patna where I was born and brought up. India's top industrialists call it their home and so do the glamour folk. I was not a stranger to the city, though. I'd visited it earlier with my brothers on a pleasure trip when my father was alive, our wallets bursting with money, courtesy of our doting father. We dined at five-star hotels, bought expensive stuff and then flew off to Goa for more fun. I was escaping my spiritual travails at that time. But this time, I would battle real problems, finding the hard way how difficult it is to earn your living on your own when your dad is no longer around to hold your hand.

I was enamored by the sea and was thrilled the first time it seemed to materialize out of nowhere when my taxi came down the flyover at Nariman Point, the city's business district. I don't know why—maybe it offered me a sense of freedom because it stretches boundlessly, maybe it gave me a sense of power so mighty it seems. At night, I just loved to sit by the shore and look out into the sea, just like that, the cool breeze gently touching my face.

This time, when I'd no free time, I would often walk by the seaside at night and wonder—How do people just sit and chat? They seem to have all the time in the world while I'm always busy, planning my next move, my career. Then, sometimes, I felt like sitting there too, just like that, doing nothing, but arise I must because I'd come here to build my career, become a star and not waste even one precious moment.

I met that movie star as soon as I reached Mumbai. He lived in a sprawling bungalow in upmarket Juhu. He acted funny right from the beginning. When he asked me to sit, I tried to sit right next to him, but he rudely commanded, "Not here. Sit there," indicating the sofa kept at some distance. Then he asked on his own, "So, you want to be an actor?" I thought this was my chance and was enthusiasm personified when I blurted out, "Sir, not only an actor, a star like you." He apparently didn't like it because the next thing he said was pretty hurtful, "You guys land up from nowhere in Mumbai and feel you can be movie stars. Have you been to Churchgate and seen how smart those guys are? You've got some nice hair, so you feel you could be the next idol like Mr Anand. Wake up, it's not Patna." "But sir, I'm a fantastic actor. Maybe you could introduce me to some director, you know so many," I insisted. "Kid, I never sought help from anyone when I came here, and I don't help anyone. If you want to try your luck, do it yourself. And then movies are not doing well and who knows what happens to this industry," and blah, blah, blah, he ranted. I knew this guy would do nothing, and I would need to try out on my own and had no misgivings—I trusted my talent and my looks and was sure I would make it on my own.

University life was fun, and I made many friends. Girls

discussed who this hunk was and sought opportunities to introduce themselves. Hot blood coursing through my veins, I felt attracted to the really voluptuous ones. And then I came across two busty Russians, exchange students from Delhi University. I was leisurely walking in the night—I was living in the dorm now—and saw these babes strolling as well. I was quick to introduce myself, "Hey, I'm Arjun. You two not from the dorm, I believe?" When I show interest, no chick denies. Pat came the reply, "We are from Delhi. Exchange students. I'm Luiga and she's Liena." "Glad to meet you all," and I shook hands. We then walked together for quite some time, talking about this and that. We were good friends by the time we went back to our rooms—in India, girls and guys, sadly, live in separate dorms.

The moment I was in my room, this guy barged in, "Hey, Arjun, so you're back!" I knew this guy because he was from the dorm too and would often spin yarns about how many girls he had gone to bed with. None of us really believed him or even cared. So I was quite dismissive, "Yeah, went for a walk and now, if you could excuse me, I want to sleep." "Hey, who were those babes you were with?" he questioned, and I was really irritated, "None of your business and now, just get out." "But we've a great chance. I know some shacks we can take them to. These foreigners are so hot," he drooled. I laughed, so funny it was, "Dude, I met them just now, and you think they will be ready to bed? And by the way, how do you get invited? If I wish to do something, I'm man enough. Why do I need you?" "But there are two of them," he persisted. "And you think I can't handle two," I said, my eyes shining with mischief and threw him out of my room.

To tell you the truth, I would love to make love to many of

those hot chicks, but something restrained me. The moment a girl started getting close, I shied away. Maybe I feared commitment, maybe I was plain scared of catching some disease. I would typically wonder, "This girl is getting too close and might even be willing to go to bed with me. But, then she might've been so with others as well, and what's the guarantee that she's safe?" It was fear again, that enemy of mine that was restricting me from something very natural for a young man. And what was the guarantee that any young woman cozying up to you is only interested in sleeping with you? Some wishful thinking that! My friends would encourage me, "Bro, don't think too much, just take her to bed." And I would nod in agreement but would do nothing of the sort.

I made a friend in the dorm, Rags. He was shy and quite introverted. His elder brother assisted some director in the south, and he was quite dismissive of movies, "Pal, it's a bad field. People just promise and never do anything. They only sell dreams, nothing more." I was not listening because I'd no way out. Business back home was faring poorly, and I'd no hope it would recover, and Patna offered no alternatives. I could not think of the IAS now as I was overage and the same went for an MBA—I tried this option too! At that time, MBA courses in India were weighted in favor of fresh graduates unlike in the US where experience was considered valuable. So, the only way out was the movies, and I was quite sure I would make it.

Some of the mates in the dorm were pursuing similar dreams, and they encouraged me no end. We even did a photo shoot in a shabby studio. Much later would I realize how tacky those pictures were—my face was powdered, eyebrows made bushy with a black eyeliner, and lips, red with lipstick. Seriously, who really cares for such cheap stuff—I would get a professional photo shoot done much later and understand what good pictures were.

There were some weird characters in the dorm. There was this guy who claimed to have topped some provincial civil services exam but did not deem it fit to join some of the lucrative jobs these offered. He claimed to be a director, producer, writer, and whatnot but shamelessly imitated the reigning superstar. If he wanted to act why couldn't he simply admit? Wonder of wonders, he used to go to poop with his boots on and apparently none had ever seen him take a shower. He was quite appreciative of my physique though and kept encouraging me to become a film star.

Then there was another guy who aspired to be a movie star too. He was quite short and ordinary-looking but believed he could swing things his way in some artsy kind of films.

One evening, as I was entering the lobby of my dorm, he called out to me, "Hey Arjun, how are you doing?" "I'm fine, and what about you?" I replied casually. "I'm fine too. There's something I want to offer you," he said and then, looking at the quizzical look in my eyes, he continued, "How would you like to play the lead in a play?" I was pleased with the offer, "Why not, I'd love to. Who's directing it?" "I'm directing it," he replied. "Oh," I said, a little disappointed because I felt it was going to be an amateur production, not a professional one. But I was still interested because I never wanted to let go of any opportunity to perform and enquired, "What's it about?" "Well, it's going to be a kind of musical where a bunch of boys pursue a girl, but it's you who gets the girl," he answered. I was horrified, "A musical? You mean I will need to sing?" "Of course! Dude, why not use your baritone!" he mischievously replied. "Okay, I will," I signed off, not too interested.

We rehearsed every night, and the play turned out to be really nice. I still remember the catcalls from girls in the audience. For a few days after that night, I kept getting furtive glances from girls who admired my performance but couldn't express openly, so typical of an Indian girl of that time. I thoroughly enjoyed the adulation and only wondered what promise the film industry had in store for me.

CHAPTER THIRTEEN

I started visiting movie studios, and folks out there seemed to like me, asking me to leave my pictures with them. "Dude, we will call you the moment something interesting turns up. We don't want to waste your talent with something small," they promised, and I was so revved up, "Here's my chance and no one can stop me." On one of the shoots I visited, the lead actress just couldn't take her eyes off me. When I walked on the road, people seemed to notice. And I was deadly in a body-fit tee—people just stared and stared.

One of the casting directors—we were talking on the phone—asked me pleasantly, "Son, when you walk on the road, do girls notice?" I was a bit cocky when I replied, "Well, they just can't take their eyes off me!" And he was quick to invite, "Okay, do drop in with your pictures." When I reached his office, however, after a longish, circuitous route in a crowded bus, all he had to offer was a bit part with the promise that I would get something bigger in the next project. I was not interested at all because I was looking for lead roles only. I soon realized that getting the lead was really difficult. When they inquired what role you were looking for and you answered, "Sir, I'm looking for the lead," they'd be shocked, wondering whether you were nuts. Only those from the film fraternity or the ones with bags full of money could land a lead role. I had neither and hence, was a lost case to many.

Then someone suggested, "Why don't you join this elite acting school?" "Why, I'm a born actor! What can anyone teach me?" I was indignant. "Someone could just offer a chance. This particular teacher taught many of the stars who dominate the movie industry today," came the reply. I was skeptical because many struggling actors at one of the famous meeting points had told me nothing really happened, "Bro, no one gives you a chance. It's better you go back to Patna. You will only be wasting your life here." When I told the famed teacher what I was hearing, he was dismissive, "You've been talking to failures. Do my course and see the magic."

The course was pretty expensive, though. I was clutching at straws because I'd already left my business, and the only way out was to go ahead and find something that worked. I had no money and had to request my brothers and Karan was quick to respond, "Don't worry. I will send you the money." My mother was to tell me later with what difficulty he used to organize the money to indulge my fads.

Acting school was fun, though. The first day I got to perform with a hot chick—spotless complexion with a dainty waist and curves at all the right places. It was a longish scene from one of the classics, and my performance was fantastic. The teacher was quite impressed while the boys were jealous. I looked forward to performing with the cutie the next day, but she joined another batch! Apparently, she was tired of performing with so many boys as she was the only girl in my batch.

When I was acting, I was extremely instinctive because it's my belief that if you're blessed with the superstar quotient, it will shine through when you ride your feelings. If you feel constrained by anything—be it the burden of expectation that what you deliver has to be a masterpiece or when you seek to please, be it the audience, your director or anyone else for that matter, your creativity is gone because your instinct is no longer unfettered, and you will fail to expand like the open skies, resulting in a poor, mediocre performance. But then, that moment before the camera is yours. So ride your instinct for sure but also own that moment, create in that moment and watch what magic unfolds. As I'm fond of saying, "An artist walks a tightrope. While I've my artistic freedom and I'm not trying to please anyone, yes, I'm trying to impress as well because that's my moment and I may not get the opportunity again." I'm not being pessimistic when I say you may not get a chance again, it's being realistic. Ask any struggling actor how difficult it is to get a chance to perform and you'll get what I mean.

When you're handed the script, don't finish reading it until you understand it perfectly. Your concentration, again, will hold when you read instinctively. I would teach my students later the art of reading comprehension—Be at ease before you read; if there's something to be figured out, stop and figure it out before you proceed so that once you've finished reading the given passage, you can sum it up in your own words. And what tells you you've understood the scene perfectly—you guessed it right, your instinct! How much of my teaching later would be inspired by instinctive acting! I can't overstate the priceless lessons I learned then. I also believe that you should never launch into a performance until your instinct tells you you're ready for the take because only then will you flow effortlessly into the role.

My teacher found me annoying at times because I always waited for my feelings to give me the cue. But my acting was fantastic and my teacher soon started loving my eccentricities. My classmates were extremely jealous and tried to misguide me, "Oh, you're just copying the expressions of Mr Beacham! Copycats never succeed. You must do something of your own." When I told my teacher which particular superstar they alleged I was imitating, he was amused, "Son, at this young age you're being compared to such an icon. What more can you ask for? Just ignore the jealous lot with contempt."

He handed me letters of recommendation glowing with praise especially highlighting my mastery of emotions. On cloud nine, I enthusiastically met several producers and directors. There were promises galore but no work forthcoming. But I was getting money from home and was not dispirited. And then happened one of the best performances of my life. It was a huge monologue from one of the blockbusters, and the performer was the phenomenon, the biggest superstar of all times, Mr Beacham.

The teacher handed over the script to the whole class in the evening and asked us to perform the next day. I read the script that night and rehearsed once. The next evening, I went for the performance. The class was spellbound, and the claps were just not stopping. My teacher was awestruck, "You had been practicing for long!" "No sir, one rehearsal and now the take," I replied nonchalantly. "Brilliant, stupendous!" my teacher sang. My classmates told me I had surpassed even the megastar with my performance. I was ecstatic—Superstardom, you just wait; I'm coming! The prince is on his way, ready to get anointed!

I kept attending lectures at the university meanwhile because I'd to retain my dorm room. I always had girls for company, and they were all so interested. I was not losing sight of my goal though because it was the only career I was left with. We often had coffee at the college cafeteria, and one such afternoon, something momentous happened.

CHAPTER FOURTEEN

As usual, I was with some pretty chicks, and we were talking. I casually remarked, "Viji is quite liberated in her outlook, just like those in the West." Now, this was one really hot babe that you would like to date. "What about Isha?" someone enquired. Now, Isha was this innocent, cultured beauty whom you dare not flirt with. You try to flirt, and you'll get a contemptuous snub. I was quite dismissive, "She's just too simple. Not the type we are talking about." All of a sudden, I noticed she was teary-eyed and wondered what I had said that should hurt her. But I let it go and thought no more of it. I was quite clear—I am here to become a star and not get into any kind of relationship, least of all any kind of commitment with someone so emotional. Flings were fine, though even here I was not very interested because my career was primary, every other thing could happen later.

But, unknowingly, I was getting dragged into a relationship. A friend of mine broached the topic, "Both Isha and you are so bright. Why don't you all marry?" And then, sipping some delicious coffee, he would continue, "Do we have an east-west marriage on the cards?" (I came from Patna, the eastern part of India and she from Mumbai, western India.) I was quick to dismiss any such possibility, "No, no, not at all. I'm not here for marriage." Again, tears in her eyes and the thought lingered in my mind, "What's the matter? Is she getting attached to me?"

A couple of days later when I was attending a lecture, a friend of mine called me out. I wondered what the matter was. When I went out, I found Isha waiting for me with some friends. I was surprised—Why should she wait for me? And then her friend spoke, "Arjun, she likes you and wants to marry you." I was shocked because marriage with anyone was not on my agenda. I'd a one-point program to make it big in life and then let other things happen. My reply was a terse "No" and I wouldn't hear any more of it. Isha was visibly upset and wanted to talk. I said, "See, I respect your feelings, but this is not what I've come here for. I'm here because I want to become a huge star. This is my dream." She hadn't expected movies were what I wanted to do and was quite candid, "I cannot accept my husband romancing other women even if it is on screen and not real." I was quite relieved and told her, "Great. So we've no compulsions. Let's continue to be good friends."

But Isha continued to look forlorn even later, and I wondered what the problem was. Movies were turning out to be elusive too—there were promises galore but no work forthcoming. I was confused—I won't be getting this kind of a girl again if I don't succeed. Should I let her go? And, who knows, she might be touchy at the moment but later, maybe, she would be more accepting. My inexperience with girls was telling me this because I'd never been in a relationship before. The max I did was to flirt and that's all.

Then, there was an announcement on TV that people my

age were allowed one more attempt at the IAS that I'd always coveted so much. I felt it was a godsend, and I would definitely crack the exam. So dreaming, I told her, "Okay, I've given up my acting aspirations and will be trying for the IAS. If you're fine, we will go ahead." She couldn't believe her ears, "Really! I love you so much!" And a new chapter in my life began.

It seems strange that someone so wedded to films could give up that career so easily. But getting into the IAS was my original dream. Movies happened more as an escape from Patna where I saw no future for myself and again, I had no other career open because of my age. As I'd always been brilliant, I thought it was really a safer bet. And then, this pretty, cultured girl would be a part of my life, something impossible in my society where only the highly qualified, well-placed folks could aspire for such matches. People like me would get only the plain-looking rejects from ordinary families. I was not coveting anyone's money even though she was well off, but I surely wished for a match I could boast of.

CHAPTER FIFTEEN

We were a couple, and our friends kept away so that we could have privacy. I was entering a new stage of my life and was happy. But there was trepidation too—I'd no career, and marriage requires some job so that you are able to run a family. I was trying to study hard, but concentration eluded me even now. Again, irrational, baseless fears troubled me. A guy from the dorm, a civil engineer by qualification, told me how faulty the structure of the dorm building was and that it could collapse during heavy rains. I was scared that the building might cave in one rainy day and kept ruminating—my old weakness. The result was my inability to find even a bit of concentration, and it was so frustrating that I couldn't do anything about it even though I was aware that it might be the last chance that I had to fashion a great life for myself and my girlfriend. And it was so galling to see other guys from the dorm studying so hard. I hated myself for my cowardice but could do nothing at all. And can you imagine—the building still stands tall after so many years!

In hindsight, I feel that instead of giving in to vague, baseless fears, I could have just calmed my mind and allowed things to unfold. I feared that the building might collapse. I could have told myself—Okay, let's see whether this happens at all. When the building stayed strong, my fear would have vanished because no lies survive the test of truth. A crucial prerequisite here was composure because an agitated mind cannot discern and is muzzled by ruminating thoughts that soon morph into terror, making a monster of vague threats. Once it's terror, the challenge is too huge for a tortured mind, and this is exactly what happened to me. A coward dies a hundred times before he actually dies, but a brave man dies once only, and nothing could be farther from the truth. So stay calm when fear strikes, analyze it carefully, and then act. Call its bluff because fear never has any substance and survives on bluffing alone. Do exactly what it tells you not to do and watch the magic unfold. Please keep in mind that I'm not asking you to be rash, only to be courageous enough to expose fear's true colors. And no ruminating thoughts at all or you'll suffer the same fate as mine.

I lost out on a brilliant career just because I was too chicken to concentrate. I never lacked academic brilliance but if you cannot concentrate, you certainly cannot crack a tough exam like the IAS. I often wonder what kind of a beautiful life I could have scripted if I'd not given in to fear and qualified for the IAS. I surely would have avoided so much pain that I was going to endure in fruitless pursuits. And I had no right to subject my wife to such a hellish life either. How many promising lives have been snuffed out by this monster, it's hard to count, but one thing is certain—if you want not to rue your blunders later, master your fears at the earliest. Believe me, life will be really worth it once you've tamed the beast and so much fulfilling too because you will not weep for the lost chances that would stay lost forever.

CHAPTER SIXTEEN

We often went to Bandstand, a place by the sea in the posh suburb of Bandra, and stole some precious moments together in some quiet nooks as so many other couples, who could not afford expensive hideouts, did. Come to think of it, the place was quite isolated and couples, easy prey for anti-social elements. Thank God, nothing untoward happened, but I must tell all you love birds—Steer clear of such desolate places whatever be the monetary constraints, or you will be inviting trouble.

One such afternoon saw me desperately seeking a washroom. But, there were no public utilities over there. We frequented a seaside café too, but it was a cheap one with dirty washrooms. I suddenly hit upon an idea, "Well, there's a five-star hotel nearby. Why not use the facilities there?" Isha was shocked, "We don't have the money! How will we afford their expensive cuisine?" I was to shock her more, "Who says we're going to eat there? I'll just use the washroom, and we will saunter out. Who would know we didn't eat there?" She protested vehemently, but I had my way. But when we were walking out, the security officer stopped us, rudely questioning me, "How could you use the washroom when you're not a guest?" I was scared for a moment but then put up a brave face, "We were going to eat when you stopped us. How dare you question a guest?"

The officer was taken aback by my bravado, "I, I apologize sir. Sometimes we do get some undesirable elements," and wrung his hands helplessly. I feigned irritation, "And you thought we were the same type! How could you be so careless? Be careful the next time." We then went to the coffee shop and had some coffee and pastries, blowing up almost all my money. But this was the first time I had treated my girl to five-star luxury, making me really happy. Life would see many such moments later but moments planned deliberately and money spent lavishly, not under compulsion at all.

Not always could we afford to meet up at fancy joints, and some cafes near the university campus were our favorite haunts too. Now, Isha had not told her parents about me since she was unsure how committed I was. She had a cousin at the university who spotted us acting lovey-dovey at one of the cafes and was quick to inform her parents. Her parents were overly protective since she was their only child and losing no time, started investigating my background. Here I was in a soup because I was five years older than her, had no job and was an actor without any assignments. Her mother was vitriolic, "Someone who hasn't achieved anything till this age will do nothing! This chap is twenty-seven years old, and what has he really been doing all these years!" But no math predicts life correctly because life has its own permutations and combinations, and a seemingly lost case dazzles the world at times. I was very sure that I would make it big one day and, surprisingly, so was Isha.

Her parents and relatives tried their level best to dissuade her, but she was adamant. They were left with no choice but to call me home for dinner. I was a bit unsure but dressed up impressively and reached her house on time. Her parents liked my personality but felt I was quite dark—Yes, even in India people bother about the color of your skin. In fact, later, when I asked a casting director why I was never considered for a lead role, she was candid, "Such roles are meant only for fair guys. Dark chaps like you are fit only for supporting roles." A model coordinator affirmed, "Bro, you need to look like a European for lead roles. You just don't fit the bill."

I told her parents about my business background, and they were a bit relaxed. Inside, I was shaky because our business was doing really badly, and I didn't want to lie about it. But sometimes, you need to keep quiet, and I was already pinning my hopes on my attempt at the IAS—all this happened while I still had that chance that I blew up later. I sort of convinced myself that if I succeeded in getting into the elite service, nothing would really matter.

At the same time, I've always been very clear about my strengths and weaknesses and a very good predictor of my success or failure. I knew I wouldn't be able to crack this tough exam with a broken concentration—irrational fears would not let me concentrate as I've discussed earlier—and quaked from inside that I would falter. To complicate matters, Isha's parents were insisting on a formal engagement because their society was too conservative to allow girls to meet guys without some kind of ceremonial commitment. I didn't want anything formal till I was securely settled in life. I even felt that if things didn't work out for me, she could marry someone well-settled. How cruel on my part to even imagine she could get married to someone else after loving me so much! But helplessness can make you do anything, and if I could just muster the courage to trounce baseless fears—what a fantastic life would have awaited us both! Alas, if only I could conquer my fears that traumatized my whole being!

I had to bow down to her parents' insistence and took them to Patna where my family welcomed them. Now my younger brother had been paying all my bills but to my surprise, he always gave me money beforehand so that I could pay whenever my family and Isha's family went out for dinner. Of course, my in-laws were insistent that they would pay, but we didn't allow them to, as they were our guests. Her parents felt I was well off because even then my family could sustain the appearances of affluence. We weren't cheating anyone, but we were just used to the good life.

Then my in-laws broached the topic before my family, "We are really happy with the background Arjun belongs to. Whatever apprehensions we had are gone. Why not get them engaged at an early date?" My mother was ecstatic because she always wanted me to settle down, "We're really happy to meet you all too. And I too want them to get engaged. How is December for an engagement? It's just a few months away." "Yes, that would be fine," my father-in-law was quick to respond. "And let's have the ceremony in Patna," my elder brother requested.

My in-laws had no objections and from now on, my life would change for sure. I would no longer be the lone wolf striking out on my own without a care in the world and would need to find myself some secure job to run my family. Was I prepared? Would I need to wait before I found the promised land? Well, only time will tell.

CHAPTER SEVENTEEN

My university exams were over, so I had to vacate my dorm room. With great difficulty, I could find accommodation as a paying guest. My acting classes were over too, and I was meeting directors on the sly without telling Isha because I was so unsure about my success at the IAS, as I've discussed earlier—when the results were out, I'd not qualified. On my request, my teacher gave me letters of recommendation addressed to some big makers. He predicted a great future for me in the movies, but the responses were not encouraging at all. One such maker, Mr Anand, had been a romantic phenomenon as an actor when he was younger. I met him with great expectations. He looked me over and then enquired, "What kind of roles are you looking for?" "Sir, I want to do the lead," I replied enthusiastically. What followed was quite disappointing, "Son, forget leading roles. I can offer you supporting roles only." He then gave me his telephone number and asked me to keep in touch.

I then met another director, Mr Kumar, who had been revered as "the thespian" for his emotional prowess as an actor.

I was again full of expectations—This guy has been known for serious acting, no frills, no frivolities; he will certainly appreciate my awesome talent. However, the story was the usual one. He looked me over without any interest and then told his assistant, "Tell this boy I've no role for him." I'd expected to get the lead, and here he was, offering me nothing, and this was utterly disappointing.

I still was not losing hope though and performing fantastically at auditions. One such audition was conducted by an acclaimed director for a show to be aired on a prominent channel, and I was again amazing. The clapping in the room didn't seem to stop, and the director told me she would get in touch. No calls came however, and a nagging doubt started troubling me—Am I going to get anything here or are these just promises as other struggling actors tell me?

I was soon to be engaged, and then I had another outstanding performance at yet another audition and felt, "I surely will make it big. Let me not pay attention to frustrated guys." And then, full of confidence, I set out for Patna.

My engagement was a lavish affair courtesy of my father-in-law who didn't hesitate to splurge on his only child—it was after all her big day. The ceremony was held at a five-star hotel, followed by some nice food. I met many of my relatives and close acquaintances after a long time. They all seemed really happy for me, but everyone seemed to silently inquire: What's the boy doing? Does he have a good job? Many knew about my acting aspirations and knew I was getting nothing, and yet I was about to marry. "How will he afford a family?" was the sympathetic, tacit question. Throughout, I was putting up a brave face, more to myself because I'd no clue what I would really get but didn't wish to spoil my mood either. My mother was really happy and confided in my mother-in-law, "This kid of mine never got anything in life. I'm so happy that he's finally settling down with a nice girl."

A few days later, they had to go back to Mumbai, and I insisted that I accompany them to Delhi from where they were to get a connecting train to Mumbai. Since they were travelling first class, I had to travel the same way. My brother, however, pointed out that I would have to return by second class because we had no money to splurge. I hated it but had no choice and was doubly convinced that I had no future in Patna and had to make it anyhow in Mumbai, and movies were the only way out.

I was back in Mumbai, determined to make it big as an actor. My teacher was kind enough to give me letters of recommendation yet again, addressed to some big names and he especially pointed out my mastery over emotions. There were assurances for small parts but nothing big, nothing exciting. What was sustaining my high spirits was my indomitable belief that I would surely succeed one day.

Amidst all the chaos, there was a new development. The government decided to offer people my age yet another chance at the IAS exam. I was tempted and even my acting teacher encouraged me, "It's prestigious to be in the IAS, you know. Bright young men like you shouldn't let the opportunity pass." Perhaps he was dissuading me from a career in the movies because he knew so well how daunting the task was and how ruthless guys over there really were.

I knew it was a great chance to set things right—I'd compete and then marry, and life would be so picture-perfect as a top bureaucrat. I was getting a taste of how difficult it was to succeed in the movies, and here lay salvation, a gift from God. So, I decided to take the plunge. But I was again committing a mistake. I was planning to go back to Patna to prepare even though I could have done the same in Mumbai. But then, circumstances were forcing me. I had a horrid experience as a paying guest, making me feel it would be so much better if I prepped in the comfort of my home in Patna. Only my fiancée would not be there for moral support, but she would be available on the phone. Then, my mother would be there as my emotional anchor, and my brothers would help as well. So maybe it was not a bad decision at all. But, would my concentration hold and would it have held had I continued in Mumbai because there I would've always thought of getting settled in life with the support of my sweetheart?

CHAPTER EIGHTEEN

Back in Patna, I tried hard to concentrate. But again, it was a huge problem. The moment I sat down to study, distracting thoughts would start crowding my mind and like a fool, I would engage with them. My concentration would go and once it was gone, it was really hard to get it back. And I was competing against the best in the country. It was never going to be easy but with no concentration at all, it was well-nigh impossible. I would learn much later that it's really not necessary to engage with the thoughts you don't want to. Live in the moment before you and create whatever you wish in that moment because that is the only moment you have. And my present at that moment was definitely very sweet, if only because my girl loved me so much.

In hindsight, when I seem to know a few things as a teacher of some repute, it would have been so simple to just calm my mind, approach the syllabus one thing at a time, analyze it and let it be till the brain was ready to tackle more topics. And not force the brain at any time. It's my considered belief that if you let the brain be, it will serve you well. But the moment you force it, it will rebel and you'll understand nothing. So the moment attention drifts, just relax and when things settle down, gently prod it back into your work, and your comprehension will be fantastic. Again, instinct that I know so well as an actor. Read only when your brain is ready, just as you act only when you're mentally prepared, and your comprehension would be so amazing, with so much of ease. Reading is a very secondary activity, calming and stilling the brain is the real thing. As a writer, it's my belief that writing, too, is a very secondary activity. Once the mind has been stilled and the subject matter analyzed calmly, you've to just put it on paper. And writing is always a journey that one should undertake with pleasure—it never is a chore and those who consider it one, always fare miserably.

Alas! All of this was not remotely apparent to me at that crucial juncture, and I was cracking up under pressure, going crazy just before the exam. I was so ashamed of myself—Here God has given me a beautiful chance to resurrect my career; this girl has committed her life to me; and I am not man enough to perform. And my elder brother would be so angry, "You're just an escapist! What kind of a man are you who cannot handle pressure? What would come of you, God only knows!" Harsh words but true and if only I could do something, my life would've been entirely different without my being forced into fears and tears all the way through before God resurrected me.

Very predictably, I failed the exam once again and had no choice but to go back to Mumbai. My parents-in-law still believed I was trying for business and weren't unduly worried about my failure. They believed business always had much better prospects, the megalopolis always having much to do with money and full of such believers.

My parents-in-law were insisting that we get married, and I could make no more excuses. But my conscience would force me to tell Isha that our business was in a shambles, and I'd no money and didn't have much faith in my future, either. She was shocked but was too much in love to have a rethink now.

Before I proceed, I must point out my mother-in-law's kindness. When I came back to Mumbai, I'd no place to go to and no money to spend. I requested an aunt of mine to allow me to live with her till I found my feet. Now, her husband had a huge bungalow and the very same people had often stayed with us whenever they came to Patna, my father playing the perfect host, pampering them like anything. My aunt hedged, "Why don't you enroll for a doctorate? You'll get accommodation easily as the university does provide such facilities to its students." Despite my insistence, she was not relenting. My mother-in-law could sense my discomfiture and told her daughter, "Tell him not to worry. He is most welcome to live with us." This is something I will never forget.

CHAPTER NINETEEN

Back in Patna, everyone was really excited about my marriage, especially my mother who just wanted to see me happily settled in life. But there were people who were quite insensitive too. One morning, the moment I woke up, I found an aunt of mine sitting just next to my bed, and she was quite amused, "You know Arjun, I know a guy just like you. He's so eager to tell me he's getting married. But what does he do for a living—nothing really."

If it was intended to be a joke, I didn't quite get it. But she wasn't the only one to be so crude, other people were talking too and they weren't really discreet either.

On my way back to Mumbai for my marriage, this time with relatives in tow, I was quite dismayed to find everyone talking among themselves, none really bothered about me even though it was my wedding they were going to attend.

Isha's friends were pretty inquisitive too, "You're getting married, but what does he really do? He's supposed to be an actor but he's nowhere to be seen. Are you sure you're making the right choice?" Her relatives were quite annoyed that I was from a different community. My parents-in-law, however, were quite ecstatic that their only child was getting married. They were under the impression that after the marriage we would settle in Patna where, supposedly, my business was flourishing.

The wedding was a lavish affair courtesy of my in-laws, but my financial problems loomed large. To recount an incident, it's customary for the bride's female cousins to hide the groom's sandals and then ask for some money before they return the same. They asked for two hundred bucks, and that's all I had in my wallet.

Back in Patna after the wedding, we had a lavish reception. But people had become openly insulting now. The first question to the bride from some of the cruelest cousins of mine was, "What, after all, did you see in Arjun that you agreed to marry him?" Supposedly, I was a total waste, one who would do nothing in life. My wife, however, was made of sterner mettle and a staunch believer, "He will certainly do well and hit it big one day," a belief that I found hard to believe myself at times.

We then went on our honeymoon to Manali, all expenses paid by my in-laws. We were happy but didn't really know where life would take us. We shopped and shopped, blowing up all the money. Mom was quite aware of my financial travails and admonished me, with a lot of concern the moment we were back home, "You should have saved money for your future needs."

Isha wanted us to live in Patna, but I knew there was no future there. Try I must in Mumbai, and the only option I had was a resounding success in the movies. Isha was hurt by the very thought that I would be romancing women on screen, and had I not promised her I would do business and anything else but not movies? I remembered everything but could find no alternative and then, the barbs, the consensus among all the relatives except my mother and younger brother that I would do nothing in life—how painful, how damning! I had to escape and become something in life, come what may.

I forced Isha to call her mother and tell her we would be back in Mumbai, which shocked her because it's quite unusual for the daughter to come back to her parents' house after marriage and this time, with her husband in tow. But she had no choice, and I lied that I was coming back to explore business opportunities. A typical middle-class family in Mumbai would be quite dismissive of films where only the well-heeled succeed, a thought that was fully justified and that I'd concede after much pain.

CHAPTER TWENTY

If wedding is bliss, we weren't able to experience it. Each day brought more pain and constant worrying. People in the building were curious, "What does this guy do? He's always home!" My wife's friends asked her whether I bought her new clothes because a close friend of hers, who had also got married recently, apparently had much to show off. I was trying hard, but movie roles were so hard to come by. Casting directors would say they would call when "a suitable role" happened, but there were no calls. My struggle was hard—walking a couple of kilometres under the blazing sun before catching a bus, then getting down after a crowded mindless hour near production houses, and then keep walking for hours, begging for a role at every door.

The cruelest thing about many filmmakers in Mumbai is that they never tell you not to come. They will always say, "Have patience, keep meeting. There might be something for you, if not in this project, then definitely in the next one." And you keep going with hope in your heart only to be disappointed again, and again, till your hair start greying, and they start avoiding you. I knocked at the door of one such producer for four years and he always assured me, "Son, have patience. I will definitely have something for you." Sadly, that day never came.

My mother-in-law was getting restive, "If he's not getting business here, let him go back to Patna where his family business is doing so well." My lies were coming back to haunt me, and I was clueless about my future.

Then, all of a sudden, I got a small part in a TV show for which I had to travel to Rajasthan. I had no money to travel and asked my wife to take a loan from her mother. When her mother asked what the need was, she was forced to lie, "He's on a business trip to Rajasthan. We'll repay the moment he's back."

The journey to Rajasthan was quite uncomfortable—I had to travel second-class by train, and it was dusty and hot. I was then whisked away to some very ordinary accommodation in a village where shooting was going on. I then experienced first-hand how fickle and untrustworthy movie guys were—the role I had been promised had already gone to someone else, and some bit part awaited me. I prepared well to perform even though I was quite disappointed. I was facing the camera for the first time professionally, but even then I delivered the few lines given to me with panache. My co-actor was a seasoned artiste but was so incompetent that there were many retakes. I was scared I might run out of steam by the time the shot was ok'd but, thankfully, things went well, and the director nodded in approval, asking his assistants to call me again. He was quite surprised when I told him, "Sir, this is the first time I faced the camera professionally," and I felt elated—My time starts now; I would definitely be a star.

I was quite surprised when people felt how lucky I was

to have shot two episodes that day, translating into twice the money I would have earned otherwise. The payment was quite meager, and I would rather congratulate myself on having performed so well—I would learn later, to my utter dismay, that every penny was important when you'd to eke out a living in the movie industry, and many would be ecstatic with the measly sums they made rather than artistic fulfillment. Would I give in and accept that pathetic lot as my destiny, or would I seek deliverance elsewhere—this would be the big question that held no clues for me at that time.

CHAPTER TWENTY-ONE

I was quite curious to know how people would react when my episode was on air and just didn't know how to divulge the secret to my in-laws. Then one day, I just blurted out, "I will be on television." My in-laws were shocked as this was something they wouldn't have dreamt of ever. However, when they saw me act they liked it and felt I might have a future in the movies. I was ecstatic when I got another role because some casting guy liked me on the show. But, the problem was they were all bit parts, and such roles typecast you as a small-timer. Anyways, this thought never crossed our minds at that time—the future seemed rosy.

I kept meeting people, trying to convince them I had the wherewithal to be a star. I was fed lies that when you were seen again and again, even in the bit parts people would offer, you get stellar roles later—there were so many stars who started small, after all. But the harsh reality was that you were offered big roles either through connections or when you were rich enough to invest in their projects. Strugglers like me, who would commute by public transport and then walk for hours in the blazing sun, would remain strugglers.

There was no money coming, and my mother-in-law started complaining, "What would come of this guy, he's always home!" My wife's friends started making fun of her, "Your husband doesn't buy you new clothes? Look at Payal, how expensive her dresses are." Now, Payal's husband was a rich businessman.

I was quite clueless about what I was supposed to do. No one offered me work, and I'd pinned all my hopes on this. And where could I go just like that when I'd no money and commuting was not cheap? And what was the point in rushing to production houses when no work seemed to come my way? I was going for auditions and delivering powerhouse performances. There were claps and claps, but when I asked the director, "Sir, am I in?" my hopes would be dashed immediately, "Well, your face doesn't fit the role," and then, vague promises, "We will call once something suitable comes up."

There was one director I was quite keen to work with—I believed he made struggling actors stars. There was no particular reason why I so believed. This balding film-maker had given leading roles to newcomers, but they were either famous models or from rich families. I hounded him everywhere, but perhaps he never knew I existed. He probably enjoyed being chased by a crowd of hungry strugglers. Chasing him was an excuse too for guys like me—at least we showed our families some kind of engagement rather than twiddling our thumbs at home amidst scorn and rejection.

One such afternoon, I was waiting to meet this guy. It was crazily hot and there was no shade—the cabin he was in with some star was out of bounds for strugglers. At times, he would come out, look past me and go back. I'd decided I would not budge until I met him. Then, one security guy came over, enquiring, "What's your business, buddy? Why have you been standing here for so long?" I humbly spoke, "Sir, I'm waiting for Mr Menezes." The security guy went straight to the director and told him what transpired. The director callously replied, "I don't even know this guy and never told him to wait. He just keeps following me for work." I was so sad. I had been waiting for hours in this kind of heat because I felt he would take note of my dedication, and all I got was this, this summary dismissal with such utter disregard. I now feel he was some kind of a sadist who took pleasure in being hounded by jobless strugglers, only to dismiss them with ruthless nonchalance the moment they felt there was some hope.

Despite all the disappointment and contempt, I was persisting with my choice of career. One reason was I'd nothing else to fall back upon but, even more, was my faith in my awesome talent. The moment I was handed my dialogues, I would get into the skin of the character and then, purely guided by instinct, which would somehow magically electrify my emotions, I would deliver a fantastic performance. While performing, I would automatically add my own lines too, because seldom were the lines given anywhere near perfection, and I'm a perfectionist to the core. A writer remarked, "Bro, you always add your own lines beyond the dialogues I've written, but whatever you do is amazing, and I really don't mind."

I was always waiting for that one big chance that would catapult me into stardom. Then, it so happened that the same director, who had ignored me so much, offered me a small role in a movie featuring a megastar of those days. I was ecstatic and believed something would really happen to change my destiny.

It was my first day on the sets, and I was pretty revved up.

Then the superstar turned up. One look at me and he asked the director, "Why has this guy been cast in such a small role?" I trembled—a role in a mega project after so much struggle and this guy is screwing up even that! Please, please don't do that! To my relief, the director was quick to offer an excuse, "He has a lot to do in the film. We are not wasting him at all."

In the first scene involving me, the villain was supposed to punch me hard because I'd botched up some plan of his. By the way, I was playing his henchman. He was a big, muscular guy, but I was even stronger. He sized me up, telling me he wished to be sure I would be able to take the punch if it travelled beyond the safety zone. I was super-confident about my toughness and told him, "Sir, do not worry. I'm quite strong." The shot went well, and I was quite happy, as it was my first shot for a movie and that too for a big one.

Yet another scene involving me was shot the same day. I was shown badly hurt after a fight with the lead man though the scene depicting the fight was to be filmed later. I was supposed to inform my boss what had transpired, and I was shown to be in excruciating pain. I performed so well that the director offered me another scene beyond what my role required. It was an important scene, and I was again very impressive. The director had started liking me, so it seemed.

Then came the fight scene with the lead man. He was to jump on my back, making me fall flat on my back, my head hitting the ground. I was quite scared as there was a real chance of injuring myself seriously, and I refused to do the scene. The director was livid, "How dare you refuse! You'll have to do the scene." I still refused, and he ordered me out of the film. Thus ended my first outing in the movies on a sad note.

The star, however, was sympathetic, and I kept visiting the sets to meet him in the hope that he would recommend me somewhere. One afternoon, I found him struggling to do a pivotal scene towards the climax in which he was challenging the don. I asked him politely, "Sir, could I tell you what's going wrong?" He was a bit shocked because, in the movie industry, you don't tell a superstar where he's going, right or wrong, especially if he's failing somewhere. You just wait till he gets it right. And wise words coming from a struggler—no ways! He, however, was appreciative of whatever he'd seen of me and said, "Yeah, tell me." Then I explained to him that the shot was becoming monotonous because he was talking about the murder of too many people in the same breath. One of the victims was his father, and here, he could choke, tears welling in his eyes that would breathe fire the next moment, raring to go for the don's jugular, and this is how the shot would not only have variation but would electrify the audiences too. Pretty simple work if you just ride your emotions. He got the shot right in the first take and was magnanimous enough to declare before everyone then and there, "Arjun told me how to do this scene." The director laughed but did nothing beyond to help me.

Later, when I'd implore him for some work, he'd contemptuously declare, "I don't repeat my mistakes." So, casting me was a mistake even though I acted so well, just because I feared for my safety. To guys like him, bit players were cannon fodder and if something went wrong, well, who cares? You just care for a star because millions are riding on his shoulders.

Shortly thereafter, I met yet another director whom I'd known for years, right since my acting school days. At that time, he'd been considering me for the second lead that never materialized. I'd given up hope in him, but it so happened that we came face to face in a studio where I'd gone to seek some work. He was quite warm, "Dude, where have you been? You just vanished." Before I could come up with an excuse, he spoke, "Come and meet me. I've something for you." I was happy, "What role, if I'm not being nosy?" "Bro, you're a cop. Just come to my office tomorrow, and we'll talk more," and he was gone. I was fairly optimistic that he'd have something meaty for me—hadn't he been so impressed with the letters of recommendation that I carried from my teacher?

The next morning, I was in his office bang on time. But this time, his production manager talked to me, "Well, you start shooting in a fortnight, and you'll be paid a thousand bucks a day. And the costume guy here will take the measurement for your uniform." At this time, one of the assistants spoke, "Sir, why don't we offer him the role of a friend? He looks quite nice." I was pretty annoyed—The director is offering me something big, and this idiot is talking about some petty stuff. And who bothers about money—once I'm a star, money will follow. I was quite happy when the assistant was snubbed, "It's my job to see what role goes to him. You needn't worry," thus spoke the manager.

I was confidence personified when I reached the studio, going straight to the dialogue writer, demanding, "Please hand over my dialogues now only so that I'm ready when the shot is to be taken." The writer was puzzled, "But you've no dialogues. You only have to stand with other cops behind the hero." I then realized that I'd been cheated—I was only an extra, a junior artiste like so many other guys present on the set. I only had to stand in a crowd, and such people have no future. I was shocked that someone who'd promised me such a big role a few years ago could think of me so lowly now. This set me thinking—Do I have a future in the movies or am I just wasting my life here? Is there an escape for me from this rut? I must set myself a deadline and not be a disaster.

CHAPTER TWENTY-TWO

One day, during my usual excursions to the studios, I met the director of an upcoming show. One look at my pictures and he asked me to meet the producer. The producer was impressed too, and I was on. It was one of the leading roles, and the show was to be aired on a major channel. I thought my travails were over, and my performance was amazing. The director gave me a free hand and as was my wont, I would electrify the scene with my own lines too that, I felt, were necessary but the writer had not penned. This annoyed my co-actors a great deal because I was always stealing the show. The director loved me and told me, "You're brilliant. Do what you wish, I don't mind."

Then things went wrong. The producer had no intention of putting the show on air; she was just gobbling all the money the financier was putting in. After shooting eight episodes, everyone was packed off, no payments made.

I was extremely disappointed not because I hadn't been paid anything beyond daily conveyance—money was so important to me when I had to move around with empty pockets, but the real shock was the loss of a golden chance to prove myself. Money would have just followed. But such are the ways of the world, and certain things are simply beyond your control.

Then, one fine morning, I was cast as a revolutionary in a daily soap, the remuneration fixed at a thousand bucks a day. I again felt I was on the verge of hitting it big because never before had I been given the chance to act in so many episodes. "People will definitely notice my enormous talent, and doors will open of their own," I thought with soaring confidence. But there were so few dialogues for me—mostly, I was in a group of revolutionaries silently following the leader who was a known actor. I was not paid anything beyond daily conveyance, and neither were the others. When I complained, the producer callously remarked, "Strugglers like you have no future in the industry. Be happy that you get food daily. Shoot for the show and then go home." "What about the payment," I feebly asked. "I don't pay and that's why I'm different," the lady shamelessly replied. I was now furious because neither had I any future in this show nor any money.

I quit the show forthwith and demanded my dues with all my power. She then called me to her house and issued a cheque that bounced. I was called again and issued a cheque that too bounced. It became a sickening joke—calling me again and again and issuing cheques that invariably proved duds. I was so furious that one day I just charged into her house where she was entertaining some guests. "What kind of a woman are you, torturing me like this!" I shouted. She was unaffected, "Don't you see I'm with guests, and you come charging like this?" I was angrier, "Just pay me my dues, you've made me run enough, and I will not leave until you have paid." She was silent and then politely said, "Just wait in the office, I'm coming." Her office was just outside her living quarters. I went there and waited.

She came charging soon, "You dog, you insult me before my guests! How dare you!" Before I could anticipate her next move, she slapped me hard on the face and ordered her goons to hold me tight, and thundered, "Do you realize you're on the thirteenth floor? If I ask these guys to throw you down, what will you do?" I was terrified but had the sense to lie with conviction, "My uncle is the top cop in the city. If anything bad happens, you'll be in big trouble." I think I really am a fantastic actor because the bluff worked and she ordered me to be released. But there was a dark menace in her voice, "I'm letting you go today but if I find you anywhere close, you know what I can do." Thanking my stars, I ran for my dear life.

I later got the opportunity to audition for a major role in a show slated to be aired internationally on a fancy channel. The role required nuanced shades but overall, emotions of a very sophisticated kind. This role was tailor-made for me because I always soared high on emotions. The character had committed some serious mistakes in the past and this was the day of reckoning, the day when he must take his troubled past head-on and survive or crumble under the burden of guilt.

The moment I read the part, I knew I would rule. Even my teacher had commended my mastery of emotions on several occasions. I read the lines once and was ready for the take. The emotions I unleashed captivated all present and when the performance was over, there was thunderous applause, the clapping seeming to never stop. I was confidence personified and asked the director, "Sir, I'm in?" "We will let you know," pat came the reply.

I kept calling them every day only to learn that they'd already started shooting with some other actor. Not the one to give up so easily, I rushed to the studio where the shooting was on. The director greeted me warmly, "Never mind, there are other major roles too. We will call you the day you fit in." I kept meeting but nothing materialized except for some compliments, "You've a fab physique. Keep it up." It took me some time to realize that they weren't going to give me any work—they just had words for me, big, hollow words, so damaging to the psyche of a struggling youngster who had pinned so much hope on this much-hyped show.

Then, during my usual rounds of producers' offices, I chanced across a director who had essayed villainous roles very effectively. This tall, bald guy was very strong and was keen to cast only those with powerful physiques. He liked me instantly and asked, "Dude, would you like to do my show?" I was very happy and immediately consented. He then took an audition, and I was again very impressive. The role was a supporting one but he was known to give big breaks to those he liked.

A few episodes were shot with some serious action, and he was mighty pleased. Then, I was asked to do a scene where I grappled with a huge Alsatian, rolling on the ground with that beast of a dog. I was really scared and asked the director, "Sir, can we take the shots separately and then mix them with some special effects? I, I'm really scared of the dog." He was irritated, "Don't tell me what to do. Just do what I say and he's a trained dog, not a brute. So, you needn't worry." I tried my level best to control my fear but couldn't and told him the same. The director was livid, "Do you understand we will need to pack up for the day if you do not cooperate? What monetary loss the producer will have to bear just because you are so scared!" I was almost in tears and told him I was ready for the shoot. The director, however, took note of my plight and said, "You don't shoot now because you're so fearful. Dogs understand fear, and he will definitely bite now." Then he ordered, "Pack up!"

The producer must have incurred a huge loss because that day they were going to shoot my scenes only. I, of course, was chucked out and did not get to work with him again even though he was so appreciative of my physique and talent.

CHAPTER TWENTY-THREE

My struggle would've been easier had I been understood and supported at home. My mother-in-law was restive and increasingly more vitriolic, "This guy would never do anything in life! Is he young enough to struggle for something as elusive as films? And what he does the whole day—just sits around!" There was more humiliation to come, "Neighbors ask me what he does for a living and I'm clueless. I'm really ashamed of him." Then, to my wife, "You committed a blunder in marrying him!" Then a warning, "Don't go for a child till he's settled. Who will look after the kid?"

We both, my wife and I, are extremely sensitive and were deeply hurt but didn't know what to do. Forget about having a child, we both had no interest in sex under such circumstances. I was barely earning a few thousand in the whole year and had no money to spend even on my conveyance. My wife was compelled to buy clothes sold on the streets that only the poor bought while I would buy cheap shirts that would fade after the first wash. I sometimes wondered how my in-laws were so ignorant of our plight. My father-in-law was doing very well as a lawyer, and they could've made my struggle so much easier with some much-needed financial and moral support.

Once it so happened that my wife's cousin was getting engaged to her beau at my in-laws' house. Her fiancé had been invited for lunch along with his parents. I was sitting on the sofa and so were the guests. This cousin's mother was serving food and what she shamelessly did was to skip my dish and go to the others instead. This was the ultimate insult, happening only because these relatives knew about my penury, my mother-in-law discussing everything with these wretched people.

I was so hurt by repeated insults that one day I just left the house with my bag. My wife rushed out to get me back, "Don't you know you've just ten bucks in your bag? Where'll you go?" implored she, tears welling in her eyes. I'd no choice but to come back, but with a steely resolve—I will hit it big one day and then I will show all these wretches what money is! They insult me only because I've no money, but this will have to change—I will make it change!

A friend of my father-in-law knew some influential politician who was rumored to have many friends in Bollywood. When he learned of my travails, he was quick to suggest, "Why don't we approach this friend of mine? None in Bollywood can utter a word to the contrary once he commands." My father-in-law was ecstatic and so was I. But you needed good pictures when you met such a big guy. So, I was advised to have a photo session with an ace photographer but who had the money to pay for the shoot! A friend of mine, who knew the guy, advised, "Why don't you go for half a session? It'd be much cheaper." I was apprehensive, "Would he do a good job if I went on a budget?"

"Well, he's a big name and he's to look after his reputation too. He'll do a great job, don't you worry," assured he.

So, using my wife's money that she had worked hard to earn as a teacher, I went for the shoot. The shoot was a great success but something made me uneasy—I was supposed to shoot sporting a stubble first and then go with a clean-shaven look for the remaining part. But my stubble had shades of grey that shocked the photographer a bit, but he quickly recovered and ordered his make-up man, "Darken his stubble." "Was I ageing," I wondered.

I showed my pictures to the politician but like always, nothing earth-shaking happened. I was offered the part of a henchman and even that didn't materialize.

Then a friend of mine called, "Pal, there's a show on Krishna for which auditions are on. Why don't you try your luck there?" I was desperate, "Where, tell me the address quickly?" Then he told me to go to the famous Krishna temple in Juhu, and I was there as quickly as I could. The director was a Canadian who didn't seem to be impressed at all with my appearance—my looks had really deteriorated with all the struggle and continued failure—"Well, major roles are gone and some non-speaking parts are left." "Okay, but sir, let me try. I really act well," I begged. Reluctantly, he agreed and, surprisingly, handed me a couple of pages containing some powerful dialogues. I just had to speak them out, no memorizing required. When I spoke, I was a changed man—in flow, in the skin of the character, riding my instinct with consummate ease. The director was impressed and immediately offered me a major role.

First day of the shoot and I was a bundle of nerves because

my co-actor was a seasoned performer. Before the scene, I paced up and down the corridor just outside the room where the scene was to be shot, trying hard to gather my nerves, and all of a sudden I was inspired—Why the hell am I scared of this guy? I'm simply amazing as an actor and will just eat him up! Let me take the stage and the world shall see!

Breathing fire, I went for the take, and everyone was spellbound. A friend of the director couldn't suppress his curiosity, "Dude, you are simply awesome! How do you act so well?"

I would rate my performance as among the finest in my life and do you know where it happened? In the precincts of the Krishna temple and, wonder of wonders, I was not a Krishna devotee then!

When I was required to dub my dialogues, someone had misplaced my number and they were desperately searching for me. And, can you believe it, I happened to visit the same dubbing theatre to meet some director and they found me. "It's Krishna. Krishna only called you," spoke the guy in charge of dubbing and how brilliant I was—my voice was so deep and I emoted so well! People were ecstatic.

Of course, the money was good—I was paid six thousand bucks for three days of work—and it would not be a one-off case of Krishna's generosity—my whole existence would pivot around Him later.

Shortly after, I learned that a casting director I'd been meeting for years was looking for new faces for leading roles in a TV show and felt my day was made. "Buddy, you're casting fresh faces and I'm just the right guy," I said, full of enthusiasm.

"Bro, I'm looking for young talent and you're no longer young," he replied curtly. I was trembling, "Then what kind of roles do you think I'm fit for?" "Well, supporting roles that suit your age but nothing in the lead for sure," he replied matter-of-factly.

I knew I'd need to look for something else now, as my dreams of becoming a star seemed to have turned to dust. Maybe God had something bigger in store for me, thought I.

CHAPTER TWENTY-FOUR

One day, while browsing through the daily newspaper, I chanced across an ad calling for wannabe writers for assignments. My wife had always been appreciative of my writing and insisted I must go. "Maybe destiny is offering you another chance," said she. I was doubtful that anyone would give me a break, so distraught I was with repeated failures. Anyways, just to please my wife, I decided to go.

It was a longish journey by train and once I alighted, I had to cross a flyover, walking. While walking, I could literally feel—Now I'm walking into the light beyond the darkness that smothered me always, now is the transition into something bright and beautiful and this bridge signifies that.

There were so many young candidates crowding the place, but I didn't feel threatened because of my age. I was just so enthusiastic and confident when the interviewer asked me to write a movie review right there. In half an hour, I was ready with my work, and it seemed to be pretty impressive. "Okay, you're in," smiled the interviewer, "and you'll need to write loads of such reviews for us." I was ecstatic—I was finally getting work! Then he talked about money, which was quite meager, but if I wrote at least four reviews a day I'd make more money than what I was making through movies. And the cash flow seemed to be steady too, as it was a dot-com and dot-coms were ruling the world then.

My wife was happy too, "Maybe our travails are over now and, who knows, you could hit it big as a writer one day."

As I was still trying for films, my wife and my mother-in-law—yes, she seemed to be sanguine about my prospects too—took upon themselves the responsibility of watching films on television and then telling me the stories, peppered with their takes. I was writing at least four reviews every day, totaling two thousand words, alongside my daily rounds of movie studios and would've written more had that dot-com allowed me. Money was little, but there was a sense of engagement and achievement. My troubles seemed to be over.

I was on a roll. There was yet another dot-com housed in a five-star hotel that took note of my writing and offered me several assignments with very good money. Whenever I went to meet them, they used to offer coffee and cookies, and I was thrilled with all this luxury. I even began to think of joining their team full-time, and they were more than willing.

The situation at home had improved dramatically—I was no longer considered good-for-nothing. But dot-coms were like bubbles, and the bubble burst one day. I could see what was coming because I was an avid reader of some of the finest magazines in the world. But I couldn't believe my plight would continue with such a short break and told myself, "Oh my God, this can't be happening to me! My life has just started. This surely is happening only in America. India is safe." And I was at peace. But these dot-coms were funded by venture capitalists in America and when the bubble burst they were all gone in a jiffy.

I was informed that none of my write-ups were required anymore, and I again had no source of income. It was a crushing blow but try I must, and I was not getting back to square one. Then, I started looking for glossies because they were doing well and could offer me a job. I was done with films and had no intention of getting dragged into that cesspool again.

Someone then told me about a tabloid that, among other things, published stuff about movies too. When I met the owner-cum-editor of the magazine, I didn't really like him—he was quite insensitive and offered a pittance. But so hard up was I that I'd no choice. My apprehensions turned out to be true within a week—not only was he a slave driver, making his staff work for unending hours, but also very abusive. He would insult me so much that I would go down the stairs into the open and throw stones with all my raging might into the void to control my anger. Several times, I would barely be able to fight back my tears. My father-in-law empathized and advised, "Quit this scoundrel's job. You're talented and would surely find something else." But my wife and I were haunted by the specter of poverty that had been our lot for so long, and I'd no choice but to endure the pain.

I wrote the articles so well that even this monster had to praise me. His twisted sense of rewarding my brilliance was to make me proofread as well and would scold me if I missed one comma. My eyes pained so much that I finally started ignoring the pain, worsening my myopia.

Then, one morning, he casually said, "Don't come from

tomorrow." I was shocked but was too proud to protest and just walked out. It was hard to find another job, and I was despairing. Then, all of a sudden, this rogue offered me a job again. It transpired later that he'd to bring out a special issue for which he needed my talent.

Meanwhile, I came across an ad from a big-time filmmaker inviting newbie writers to join his team. I was quick to post something interesting that really impressed their panel, and I was called for an interview. I was ecstatic and so was my wife, and I declared with a lot of conviction, "Finally I'm getting my due. Our bad days are over."

The panel was curious, "How do you write so well? What technique do you employ?" "Well, it's purely instinct—you give me something, I will sit calmly, mulling, and then start writing. Nothing mechanical about it, no making drafts, no sweat. And yes, I write only till I feel like it. The moment I feel bored, I stop writing. I will resume only the next day when I'm in the mood," was my confident reply. I just knew I was the tiger in the woods, the king of all I surveyed, the moment I sat to write, fiction or non-fiction, whatever. The producer then told me, "Okay, write a story and show me. I would like to see what you are capable of. I know you have the fire to excel. If you come up to my expectations, which I feel you will, I've a job for you for sure." When I came out of the room, I was on cloud nine.

I didn't know there were petty people in the room, too. They were quite jealous of my talent, and someone informed my employer that I'd come for a job interview. The very next morning I was summoned and told very sarcastically, "So you went for a job and talked big. None really bothered and from my side, you are fired." I was shocked not at his callousness that had been so apparent all along but because I suddenly had no job. My salary was so low that I'd no savings either.

But I steeled myself and quickly wrote a story for the producer. However, I was in for another shock—when I went to meet him, I was directed to his team instead, and they were really shifty, "We already have a team of writers and we're not looking for any more." "But I was asked to submit a story and was assured of a job if my work was liked," I protested. "You were asked for just a synopsis, not a story, you misunderstood us," they shamelessly replied and then the standard excuse, "We will call if anything comes up." I could see they had pretty girls around supposedly writing stuff that they themselves might not care for. What worked was either sex or money and to hell with talent. And here I was, with no job but great hopes that were dashed to the ground.

CHAPTER TWENTY-FIVE

Destiny was propelling me towards something much bigger, much beyond the paltry sums I'd been getting until now and that too without any certainty. My wife chanced across an ad in the newspaper inviting tutors to prep students for standardized tests required for admission to undergrad courses in the US and was quick to ask me to go for the interview, but I hedged—after all, what did I know about these tests, nothing. I'd never planned to go to America and hence, had no idea what kind of knowledge was required to teach these courses. My wife was adamant, "No excuses! You're brilliant and would certainly impress. It's destiny calling you, and you shouldn't miss the chance." I always knew my wife was surer of my potential than I was and there was no point arguing.

So, with trepidation, I went to the prep center and handed over my resume. I was really smart to submit a few articles of mine as well because they made all the difference, at least in my opinion. It so happened that the interviewer, a perfect scorer from Harvard, read my work and so impressed was he that he declared, "I can't let go of someone like you even though you've no experience. Pal, I will teach you how to teach these courses. Believe me, you'll be an ace one day."

Again, someone was surer of my talent than I was, and I'd no choice but to jump on the bandwagon. Here I must say that while many Indians go by your history, Americans care about your potential and that's how magic unfolds in this country again and again. And it was this American who gave me the chance of my life.

All those selected had to undergo rigorous training before they could be certified to teach the courses. Those found wanting were to be chucked out. I was quite scared because my math was rusty and you were supposed to teach both math and English. But, unlike in the movies where everyone was eager to kick me out, here God seemed to favor me—my trainer kept shielding me while kicking others out. I really don't know why, but he just seemed to have so much faith in my potential. Maybe teaching was my true calling, and I would later do really amazing stuff that would've made my trainer proud, justifying his faith many times over.

I was freelancing and the money was little, but I was lucky to learn some really smart strategies that would stand me in good stead when I'd start on my own. And yes, the brand would help big time in establishing my credentials.

Soon, I started getting offers from other prep companies too. I started prepping students for jobs in the UK, Australia, and Canada and won accolades wherever I taught. My financial troubles seemed to be getting over even though the remuneration was nothing to rave about. But if you've gone through the humiliation that had been my lot all along just because I'd no money, you'll understand how pleased I was when my future seemed to be secure.

Then, one of the biggest prep companies in the world, who'd just opened its office in Mumbai, offered me a job with a fixed salary. The payment was much more than what I had been making as a freelancer, and I pounced at the opportunity. Folks over there were so impressed that they felt they had got me cheap. I, of course, listened when one of them confided in me but kept my feelings to myself—Mate, who gave me this kind of money ever? I feel lucky to get a package that others envy and my life starts now!

With things getting sorted, now was the time for us to go for a child, and it all seemed so simple. But there was something not quite right—my wife was just not conceiving—and we approached some gynecologist for advice. This particular doctor was quite encouraging, "Oh, it's nothing to worry about. Just bring her along for a simple procedure, and she will conceive."

We were fairly relaxed when we reached her nursing home—It's all so simple; we will be back home in the evening. She took her in and she hadn't even done any preliminary investigation. We were not aware of the importance of that diagnosis, which had been ignored so callously by her. Isha was in the operation theatre, and the wait just kept stretching. Then, the doctor called me in, "Look, I'd to do some procedure that was required, and now the bleeding is not stopping." I was in a daze when she made me sign some papers that allowed her to go for a full-blown surgery without any liability on her part. I just couldn't understand—I'd come for a simple procedure, and now there was a surgery. Then, the anesthetist came out and said, "You need to pray now."

CHAPTER TWENTY-SIX

It was all so unreal, this surely was a nightmare. How things could get so complicated without any notice! I felt like just scooping my wife up in my arms and running away but was helpless. When she sent her car for me to go to a blood bank and get blood quickly, I just gave up. It meant my dear wife was really in a critical state; otherwise, the doctor wouldn't have offered her car. And what kind of a racket was this where the nursing home didn't even have provision for blood transfusion when life-threatening emergencies could arise? And the blood bank had to match my wife's blood group, which took time, and the roads were so crowded, and all this while my dear wife was losing blood! I just surrendered to Lord Hanuman—God, I can't do anything. I just leave it to You. Do whatever You wish.

And a miracle happened. The bleeding stopped and my wife survived. When she was shifted to her room in the hospital, I was mighty relieved. Then the doctor called me, "Look, when I was operating, there were severe complications. We've to wait and watch whether she passes urine." "Doctor, what are you saying," but before I could register my protest, she dropped another bomb, "Don't interrupt and now I must tell you, she will never be able to conceive," and then she continued her rant about gynecological complications that I could hardly hear. In a matter of hours, my world had turned upside down. I never knew I was so fond of children, but when she said we never would have any, my body shook with muffled cries—I never will have a son who would have looked like me, who would have been so strong and intelligent that the world would have been forced to sit up and take notice. It's funny that you don't value something when you've it and wake up with a shock when you've lost it. I never could imagine we would be denied this blessing after so much suffering we'd undergone.

It was hard and cruel to tell my wife what had happened when she had always been so fond of kids, but I'd no choice, "Isha, I sincerely pray you get well soon. But there are certain things we must deal with." "Oh, don't you worry, everything will be fine. But why are you so upset? Don't stress yourself, I will soon be on my feet and out of this hospital," Isha went on, knowing fully well how devastated I was. Sounding upbeat, I said, "I don't harbor any fears. God is with me, and I know nothing can go wrong. And I care a damn what crap she's talking. We will consult a top gynecologist the moment I can take you home." "Hey, what's the matter? Will you tell me, please," she said, with growing apprehension. "This idiot says you'll never be able to conceive because you'd so many complications," I blurted out. Then both of us cried and cried, a helpless fury raging in our hearts—This is so cruel. We suffered so much and just when we were settling down, believing it was the dawn of a bright future for us, came this unkindest of blows. With what belief do we face our lives now? Everything seems to be so dark, so scary.

It's hard to cope when you're dealt a hard lot, when your core beliefs are shaken up, and so it seemed to be our fate now. But, later, I would remember Isha survived because I surrendered everything to God, and God would prop me up through thick and thin, and I would fight everything out. God is the light we must follow even when darkness looms large, threatening to engulf, to devour, our very existence.

Many people advised us to sue the doctor because whatever that had happened was so tragic and entirely her fault. But I was glad Isha survived and wanted nothing of her ever again in our lives. We visited some other doctors to find out whether she could conceive, but the response was always negative. We were extremely disappointed, but life had to go on. Professionally, I was doing very well, my students topping their exams and praising me to the skies. If there was something wrong deep within, I'd no clue.

Then, one day, during my lecture, I felt my mouth was too full of saliva. I drank water and started again, but it was the same thing. I kept on drinking water and talking, but how much water could I drink? I was scared excess saliva might spray into the air, and it would look very bad. As I've said earlier, I'm extremely sensitive and would feel very bad if I lost face. The next day the same thing, and again, and again, it becoming chronic and stressing me greatly. I just didn't know what to do, and it was so embarrassing. It then started affecting my work—you were supposed to lecture, to talk until you conveyed the information to the student, but how'd you do that if you were getting scared to speak lest people understand how awkward you could be? I then started to force myself to stop the flow of excess saliva while talking and the exertion was so much that I felt absolutely exhausted. Mentally, it became a torture to speak, something that I'd enjoyed so much—I had been a champion debater, an actor who wowed his audiences through brilliant performances, and here I was, finding normal speaking such an ordeal.

I was getting severe headaches too and at times would find myself freezing—it was winter, but Mumbai is not really cold, and this surprised me. At times, I would find myself really low and wonder what was going wrong. One evening, my wife and I had gone out to dine, and suddenly, when food was served, I felt like sinking into a void and just felt like going home. My wife was concerned, "Arjun, what's the problem? Why are you turning so pale?" "I don't know, I just can't sit any longer," I mumbled and felt I would collapse. Isha was alarmed and whisked me home.

The next morning, we visited our family physician who asked me to immediately consult a psychiatrist. The psychiatrist listened to me intently and then declared, "You've acute depression, and we must start medicines." I was shocked because I never could've imagined getting something like depression. My grandmother suffered from it, but I felt I was mentally too strong to get it. My wife was adamant, "You're really sick and start taking medicines from today itself." I'd no choice but to agree.

I often wonder why it is considered so embarrassing in our society to accept that you are having a mental ailment and that you need treatment. If you've a heart condition, you don't shy away. Then why this stigma if you're depressed? People feel such folks are insane and dismiss them with contempt, and this is the reason the sufferers try to hide their condition, vainly trying to put up a brave face. And depression affects you so much that it's an ordeal to behave normally—I mean, people without such a condition find it so natural to be sunny, to smile, to laugh with gay abandon. But someone depressed would feel low and even with medication, would find it an effort to be naturally upbeat—I found it really hard and would muster all my strength to smile, to show as if nothing was wrong with me, but the effort showed and people wondered if there was something wrong. The biggest problem that I continued facing was with my verbal communication.

Once, I was lecturing a batch aspiring for graduate schools in the US. It was an ordeal to talk, and I wanted to just get over with the lecture and really prayed to God there were no questions. But, as usual, some had questions to ask. Just then my phone rang and I excused myself to take the call. When I was back, I tried to explain why they were getting that particular concept wrong, and then it happened—I started getting the chills and my eyes were filled with tears; I was on the verge of crying. Through tears, I managed to offer some explanation, and the students were so shocked that they hastened to soothe my terrible discomfort, "Sir, we understand the concept very well," and I could see the sympathy they had and just hated myself for this bout of weakness.

My struggle with verbal communication would continue for years. My psychiatrist was very casual with the flow of excessive saliva in my mouth, "Why do you bother? There're so many people who spray saliva when they talk. There's nothing to be embarrassed about." "But doctor, I never had this problem. It's so recent and so embarrassing. What will people think?" I protested. Maybe I bothered too much about what people thought–I'd been like this all my life. Maybe I was overly sensitive, and the doctor was just right. Just maybe I'd have coped with the problem better, and it would not have morphed into a monster later, threatening my very life.

Folks at the office were sure there was something wrong with me, but the students were so happy with my brilliant methods that they chose to keep mum. Maybe God was helping me because all through this trauma I was able to teach well and produce fantastic results, my students regularly getting into top American universities; some would even top the world later. The doctor wanted to administer higher doses, but he also said they would've serious side effects, and I refused to take them. This could've been the reason why my suffering prolonged, because a depressed brain is just not able to produce those feel-good chemicals in sufficient quantities.

With medicines, the flow of excess saliva stopped. Now, I should've been able to talk effortlessly, but since I was still quite depressed, it was still a torture to communicate. A depressed person can't look you straight in the eye like a normal person; his eyes would be shifty, trying feebly to make eye contact that we all have been taught is so necessary for effective communication. I had to be pretty inventive at times so that the other person was not able to guess there was something wrong.

One evening, an Indian living in Switzerland dropped by to talk to me before his daughter enrolled with us for a prep course. After exchanging pleasantries, we got down to business, "So you offer quality prep? Could you tell me some of the recent scores?" he inquired. "Yes, why not. Among my students is a world topper with the perfect score, and there are many students in the ninety-eighth percentile," I replied confidently. This is funny—you ask me about my records, and I'm confidence personified; you try to belittle, and I'm a tiger, roaring, forgetting all my troubles. I really don't know from where I draw that strength, maybe God only is helping. The same thing I've noticed whenever I meet the parents the first time—they're just so impressed. But you prolong the meeting and my spirit drops and that's the reason I would keep the meetings short, making some excuses like I'm getting late for a class or something.

This guy was quite inquisitive, and I started feeling the strain, making me resort to some acting techniques. I'd examine my fingers, spin the paperweight and then look him in the eye. Sometimes, I will just close my eyes as if in deep thought and then look at him. The reason was my inability to look straight at him for even a minute, so great and exhausting was the effort. With all those devices, I'd look only momentarily at him, and he probably would not guess there was something wrong. I was grateful to God when the ordeal was over—he apparently was too impressed to find anything amiss and did enroll his daughter with us.

CHAPTER TWENTY-SEVEN

All these problems were compounded because I again had a problem with God. My entire existence revolves around God, and I've the confidence to sail through testing times because I believe God is with me. I truly believe that your power is finite and rarely enough to tackle the shocks that life hurls at you. But when you are connected to the Supreme Lord, Shri Krishna, you've the power to conquer whatever be the challenge. It may be difficult for a non-believer to understand what I'm talking about, but I'm not asking you to be bound by rituals—be limitless, shunning anything that seeks to bind you, but see to it that you're not harming anyone while pursuing what is your due. It's what I call purity of heart, and then you see what the grace of God can unfold—believe me, it's sheer bliss that nothing can rival. Remember how I rose like a meteor when I started praying to Lord Hanuman? Only when I allowed confusion to creep in, did I get disconnected and all my troubles started.

Some of you may have a valid query—Isn't God supposed to not let such things happen? What exactly is He doing when the devotee suffers so much? Frankly, I've no clue, but what I know for sure is that when one is at his lowest and has lost all hope, God steps in and the tortured soul rises like a phoenix from the ashes. My life bears an eloquent testimony to the fact, but first, let me tell you how again I'd a spiritual disconnect.

Just before I was diagnosed with depression, I'd a severe headache when I looked at an image of Lord Hanuman intently. These bouts continued later as well, so much so that I developed a phobia for anything divine. I stopped praying too. Now, whenever I'd been stressed I used to relax by invoking the Lord, but hereafter, I'd no such relief. You can imagine a pressure cooker without a safety valve, and with my depression, I was extremely stressed. Why this disconnect should've occurred in the first place, I'm not sure—I used to force myself into deep meditation and that used to be really hard on me and that could be one explanation because meditation should always be effortless as you go deep within. Then, some people told me that it was an attack by the forces of darkness when I was in deep meditation. I had again been stupid enough to stop praying to Lord Hanuman and, instead, go in for a forced deep meditative state. Anyways, the problem was very real and would persist for seven years, the toughest phase of my life, just because I felt I was without God. Financially, I was very successful, and my students were going great guns. But without God, I was lost and would be shocked to see how forlorn and hunted I appeared in the mirror.

I'd been working out all my life and I've told you what a fantastic body I had. Even through my tragedy, I had been able to do gym and maintain a fine physique. But this was going to change, for the worse. One day, a student of mine advised, "Sir, you are very well-built, but you don't really have a beach body.

Why don't you try this new thing that so many people are trying with brilliant results?" Now, I really don't understand what crap he was talking about a so-called beach body but since he had a good body too, I chose to listen and that was such a horrible blunder. What he suggested was a grip different from mine when I was doing pull-ups on the bar for my back muscles and when I tried that, my right bicep hurt a lot. Not the one to give up, I went ahead with my exercises and then, my arm started hurting a lot more. I still kept working out for days, ignoring the pain. When the pain became unbearable, I consulted a student of mine, a doctor, and he told me, "Sir, just stop doing gym. You may have torn a ligament and if you persist, you may have to go for surgery. Give it time and your bicep will heal on its own." And then, I stopped all my workouts, waiting for that bicep to heal. It was such a torture to lose all those muscles—those big shoulders, that broad back, that narrow waist—and I would watch other beefed-up guys with helpless envy. Though my wife kept pepping me up, "Darling, you still are quite muscular and look so good," I knew the reality and would avoid looking at myself in the mirror when only in my briefs—that belly would sag and I would hate the sight so much. My body had been such an integral part of my identity that it was too cruel to be deprived of it for no fault of mine, and this depressed me even more.

While all this was happening, much to my distress, some more trouble was waiting to strike.

I had been a fussy eater all my life, but my wife tried hard to make me eat whatever was nutritious and though initially resistant, I finally consented. One afternoon, she served me some partially cooked vegetables that were supposed to be very nutritious. I'd been eating that dish for quite some time and there was nothing new in it for me. But this time, I felt that food had got stuck in my throat and started coughing. Isha rushed to get me some water, but I felt the thing was still there and wasn't able to swallow. After a nightmarish few minutes that seemed like an eternity, I felt the food slide down my throat. I still don't know whether the terror was real, but I panicked absolutely.

The torture didn't stop. I started getting fearful about eating other kinds of food too, to the extent that I felt I should go on a liquid diet. This was the period when I was without God and hence, so fearful. My wife and my in-laws were so troubled that they forced me to meet my psychiatrist again. He listened to me intently but didn't counsel me. He just prescribed a medicine and then terrorized me further, "Look, you must take these pills. But I must tell you, you may not remain very sharp and your sex drive may go low." I'd been so troubled lately that I cared a damn about sex. But my brain was my asset, my sharpness the only reason why students flocked to me. If I lost my intellectual prowess, none would come to me, and I just couldn't bear the thought of financial insecurity yet again—You all have seen what destitution I'd to struggle through all my life.

I refused to take that medicine, but how do I escape food? You must eat if you've to survive but that very thought traumatized me. It was sheer humiliation to attend social functions. Everyone would offer some dish or the other, and I'd make excuses, pitching for food that I felt had the least chance of getting stuck in my throat. A student of mine, a doctor, learned about my plight and took it upon himself to help, "Sir, you eat this pastry, it's very soft." "But how would I swallow, that cream may suffocate," I mumbled. "Don't you worry, I'm a doctor, and I can handle all kinds of emergencies," he so sweetly assured.

Eating that pastry was an ordeal, but I didn't die after all. Then he made me eat a slice of pizza that I chewed and chewed till I felt it was safe to swallow and got a pat on the back. My condition, however, was not improving, and I marveled, with loads of envy, how people could eat just anything. And all my life I'd eaten everything too! So terrible, so tormented I felt.

When I look back, I feel it was all so unnecessary. What had happened was my loss of inner rhythm. When you are eating anything, you just do it; you don't philosophize how many times you have to chew and for how long, so that food gets partially digested, sliding easily down your throat. I was thinking too much just because once I felt something had got stuck in my throat and I might suffocate—the whole thing could have been a figment of my tortured imagination alone! I was quite depressed and lost without God, my sheet anchor. And when I allowed fear in, my world went for a toss.

Fear is our toughest enemy. It's often vague, forbidding us to do something, whispering in our ear, "You're in for disaster." So you don't do that and then fear warns you about other things and you don't do that either and you're caught in a web of deceit. Remember—Fear bluffs and it has no substance. Call its bluff. Tell yourself—Okay, fear tells me not to do this perfectly normal thing because I could be in for trouble. Let me do this anyway and see whether something happens. With this bold step, you take away fear's power and when you're safe, again, and again, and yet again, no terror survives. Fear always paints a terrible future that feeds on our insecurities, and the only way to breathe free is to march ahead and not cower. Believe me, no victory is sweeter and you're so free, so limitless.

The road to recovery was not easy and I felt quite

powerless—God was my power and I couldn't invoke Him lest that excruciating pain in my forehead traumatize me yet again. My mother set the ball rolling, "Arjun, you must eat Bengal gram. It helps your digestion." With psychiatric medicines, I was troubled with severe constipation and hence, the advice. "But Mom, I've to chew so much and there are so many pieces. Some of these could get stuck in my throat," I protested. "Nothing doing. You've eaten that all your life," she was adamant. Trembling, I began eating, leaving it all to my instinct, and nothing untoward happened.

Then, a friend suggested we dine at a restaurant located in the precincts of a famous temple dedicated to Lord Krishna. We went there and found a lavish buffet with so many dishes. On purpose, I tried some Indian bread that required considerable chewing before you swallowed—I was betting on Lord Krishna's power, feeling I would be safe. I couldn't invoke Him directly, but now I was in His refuge, and He would definitely protect me. Nothing went wrong. I visited again, and again, and lo, I was safe! Gaining in confidence, I started revisiting the dishes at home too, and I was safe. The process was tedious, but the results came faster as my confidence soared and my instinct got into gear. A time came when, by the grace of Lord Krishna, I was able to eat everything that I liked. How liberating it was to be unbound, to soar free in the open skies!

Now, what could have worked here? I truly believe it was Lord Krishna's grace alone that liberated me from fear. A more mundane explanation would be: I felt safe on God's land, finding my inner rhythm and the moment my instinct started working, everything was fine because I really never had any problem with eating, something purely instinctive. It was all so unreal, assuming diabolical monstrosities just because fear paralyzed my instinctive responses.

A cousin of mine, who is a respected psychiatrist with fancy degrees, was actually quite alarmed when I consulted him during my ordeal, making me realize how terrible such eating disorders are thought to be. But believe me, if you seek God's grace and bask in His warmth, you will be delivered as I was. Free of fear, you'll find your inner rhythm and unless you've a physiological condition that needs corrective measures by a qualified doctor, you will be fine. And if you've a medical condition, still there is no need to fear—believe in God and let the doctor take care. You'll be surprised how much healing occurs when you surrender to God's care—it's sheer magic.

CHAPTER TWENTY-EIGHT

My mother was a really nice person and mentally very tough. Severely diabetic, she was unfazed—when you tell her something might go wrong with her because she had such a serious condition, she would calmly question, "Okay, then what?" She was calling fear's bluff and hence, not scared at all. Nothing could really trouble her—I mean, the kind of imaginary fears that always overpowered me. I wish I had her courage and I sometimes wonder—Both my parents were so tough, how could I be so fearful?

My mother was staying with my younger brother and was taken care of, but she was extremely fond of me and would often tell me, "Arjun, I want to stay with you. You're so intellectually inclined, I feel so happy talking to you." I was, however, staying with my in-laws because you need to be financially very strong to buy a house in an upmarket neighborhood in Mumbai—I wouldn't settle for something lowly. Well, I'm like that. And I was mentally so troubled. My wife just didn't feel secure enough to venture out. We didn't even have a car and some of my relatives—I don't wish to discuss them as they were so callous—who never did anything for us, would pester us so much. My wife was so stressed she developed a cardiac problem that, thankfully, got resolved on its own. I helped Mom financially as much as I could but failed to buy a house for her.

She was my emotional support, my friend, with whom I discussed so much. When she passed away, I was so devastated and the only support that held me together was Krishna's grace that seemed to tell, "How are you lost when I'm with you," and it would be this blessing that would resurrect me ultimately.

My mother was so childlike. She would feel happy when my wife would buy her clothes, when I would take her to a café where she would invariably insist, "I want that cold coffee with ice cream," and would have her way despite my reminders that she was diabetic. While shopping with us, she would say, "I'm feeling thirsty. I will have some cold drink," and all the beverages she liked would be laced with sugar. I would tease her, "Mom, why don't you try some water if you're so thirsty," and she would feel so irritated. She would watch movies in the theatre and I feel so happy we took her to watch whatever she wished to, just before she passed away so suddenly. And then, she would go to shopping malls and comment, "Why are these girls so scantily dressed," looking at other shoppers. I would be so mischievous, "Mom, that's the reason guys are here," and she would laugh and I would love all those moments.

My problem with verbal communication would continue. Though I was not troubled any more with the flow of excess saliva while speaking, I was fearful of people now. It defies logic to be scared now because the original problem had vanished and no longer was there a chance of losing face. But this irrational fear continued to dog me even though I tried a lot to break free. I found it really hard to share my knowledge with my students and felt really sad when fear trapped me in a web, not letting me speak freely. It seemed as if I was pressing the accelerator hard while at the same time, the brakes were on. The result would be terrible wear and tear and this exactly was happening to my psyche. If I tried too hard, my eyes would strain and I feared I might damage some nerve. Any kind of communication in public was a torture, the worst being teaching, and this was my livelihood, worsening the situation manifold. How ridiculous it was that I started fearing physical harm but failed to convince my brain that it would happen only through fear that had no basis at all.

And one fateful day, that dangerous meeting happened that nearly wiped out my career and threatened my very life. I was meeting another teacher at a café because he wanted to get into a partnership with me, "Look, we really can do wonders as a team. You're great at English and I'm very good at math. None can really compete when we come together," he tried to convince. "But I'm good at both English and math and I don't see a reason why I should surrender any of these to you," I objected. "The reason I agreed to a meeting is that you're good at counseling and I've no such experience. The way I look at this partnership is, you take care of counseling while I teach," I continued. He started objecting and then suddenly, I was paralyzed with fear, fear squeezing the nerves at the back of my neck mercilessly till I felt I would not be able to breathe, "Oh my God, I must have damaged a nerve," I felt so terrified. And amidst all this torture, I kept a serene face lest the guy feel there was something amiss and I lost face. How stupid of me, how sad, how terrible! And then

I started rubbing the back of my neck vigorously, but this guy was oblivious to my plight and kept yakking. It was with great difficulty that I ended that meeting. My neck was hurting terribly and I couldn't move it. When I told my wife she was alarmed, "Let's go to the doctor immediately!"

We had to wait for quite some time as the doctor was busy, and I was so terrified, "Some terrible thing has happened," I kept repeating. Finally, the doctor called us in and took an X-ray. He was quiet then, and I was so apprehensive. When he finally spoke, it was terrible news, "The curvature of your upper spine seems to be lost." "You mean something major," I almost sobbed. "Well, yes, but I will prescribe some medicines and you meet me after a few days," he said. The moment I was home I called up my uncle who's a doctor, and he was alarmed when I told him what the doctor had said but then was dismissive of his claim, "Had this happened you wouldn't be able to keep standing. He's talking crap," and that reassured me a bit.

It would be a very painful wait before my neck would move freely and all the pain would disappear. But I would be very, very scared—Suppose something like this happens again! I've to keep meeting parents, and they've so many questions to ask before they enroll their kids with me. They just keep talking. And then they insist on periodic meetings to get an idea how their kids are doing. Suppose terror strikes again—What will I do? I can't just stop conversing, as it would look so bad. And this time, the damage could be permanent. I may not escape.

The situation had turned so bad that I almost wished I'd no more tutoring. And my neck hurt so much when I was compelled to talk. Luckily, some parents weren't able to guess my fear of talking, feeling I must've slept badly to get that pain in the neck. Some were rude, "Enough of your problems. We've paid you and our kids can't keep waiting. You'll need to come." Again, none could figure out what mental trauma I was going through. My job was to talk and that terrorized me—then, what was I supposed to do? And I'd seen so much financial turmoil—I just couldn't imagine getting into that poverty again. I missed God so much. This was the period I couldn't pray and felt so powerless, so helpless.

When I reflect, I feel I should've been very calm when I was talking to that guy. When you're calm, your feelings are under control, and you do not go haywire. Even if fear strikes, as it did in my case, it cannot persist because you're not agitated at all. You will feel troubled, no doubt, but fear will not escalate into terror. After some time, your brain will figure out that there really is no reason to be scared—after all, that guy was not pointing a gun at me. He was just talking, some parts of which may not have been agreeable to me. I could've heard him calmly, expressed my reservations and the meeting could've gone on uneventfully. Maybe because I was depressed, I was more prone to fear and, caught in a web of passions, my mind just froze.

Now, moving on to the spiritual plane, I will tell you how ridiculously easy the solution was that, sadly, I was not aware of at that time and even later until Krishna enlightened me. I have a picture of Krishna and at the back of that picture, the Hare Krishna mahamantra is written: Hare Krishna Hare Krishna Krishna Krishna Hare Hare Hare Ram Hare Ram Ram Ram Hare Hare. One momentous evening, when I was looking at His picture in utter despair, He seemed to point out the mantra to me and, taking the cue, I started reciting the mantra. I could do the recitation 11 times only in the beginning but later, I could chant the mahamantra 108 times every day, and it was magic! The mahamantra has magical energy that drove away all the inner darkness, making me calm and poised, and I could converse with aplomb, anytime, anywhere. Once again, I was the tiger with the roar, people marveling at my rich baritone. And the mahamantra would keep me extremely positive, not allowing any negative, ruminating thoughts, driving my depression away eventually.

The magic of the mahamantra makes me ponder: Would I have been telling a different story had I known the Hare Krishna mahamantra in my troubled teens, a story of all things bright and beautiful—the radiant sun, the ethereal moon, the majestic mountains—instead of a tale full of pain, tortured tears, and morbid fears. But such are the ways of the Almighty and we can do nothing about it.

CHAPTER TWENTY-NINE

I was in for one more shock immediately after the episode I just discussed. My psychiatrist had been insisting that my medicines taper off because I'd been taking them for many years. And I was pretty rattled with the trauma I'd undergone. But when I met him, I was in for more trouble. "Look, you have been taking this particular medicine for many years, and it must go, but gradually. It could induce diabetes, though," he ranted. I was stunned—Why should I take some medicine that could induce diabetes? And how cruel of him to tell me so when I was in such a terrible state! He could have just said I needed to stop that medicine and not discussed such a serious side effect. People so badly depressed as I was, are already very scared. What's the need to traumatize them further?

When I reached home, I was so scared that my ribs started hurting. Later, I would be so fearful that it seemed my ribs would crack. My left hand would go numb. When I called up my mother—she, thankfully, was very much there at that time—she was courage personified, "What's so terrible even if you get diabetes? I've had diabetes for so many years and I'm doing fine. You just need to go to a good doctor and take medicines regularly."

Now, again, it was an unwarranted case of terror. Had I been calm, I would have been able to reason—First of all, the doctor said that the medicine could induce diabetes. It didn't mean it surely would. And then I could be off medicines before anything bad happened. He was not God either. I could go in for a second opinion. In the worst case, even if I got diabetes, there were medicines to take care. So many people lead normal lives with medicines. Again, because it would be drug-induced, maybe it would go once the drug stopped. What was I gaining out of fear—I could be in for real trouble with so much fear. People die with so much stress.

Even now, I was unable to pray as I was still without God. One night, I could bear the pain no longer and, sobbing, bowed before Krishna, my head at His feet and lo, there was magic! The excruciating pain suddenly disappeared, my head was clear, and I thought of meeting my family physician, someone very respected for his knowledge, for a second opinion. The moment he heard what the psychiatrist had said, he blurted out, "This medicine won't induce diabetes even if you take it all your life. Only steroids induce diabetes and it isn't a steroid." I was so relieved, I can't tell you. This was the second time I'd surrendered completely to God and I'd not been disappointed—first, it was Lord Hanuman and now Krishna, the Supreme Lord. I knew my bliss would begin as Krishna had taken me under His grace.

It was New Year's Day and I decided enough was enough—I must find God again and then only my redemption would begin. Quaking from inside because of the past association with pain whenever I invoked God directly, I went to this magnificent temple of Lord Krishna in Juhu. Big queues of devotees greeted me and when I entered the sanctum, there were so many people inside that I feared there would be a stampede. But then, I looked at Krishna and He said—Come to Me and do not fear. Your life will be beautiful. And then there was more of grace that calmed me completely. Suffice it to say that I was a changed man after that experience and would not cower even when I was challenged by circumstances beyond my control later. I would completely be in sync with Krishna, surrendering everything to Him, firmly ensconced in the Krishna mindset. It would be a steady rise in my fortunes and a rosy future would beckon.

My medicines would taper off with the faith in a secure life, and I would be on the lightest of medicines possible, my psychiatrist extremely impressed with my serene countenance and the confidence I exuded.

The problem with verbal communication didn't disappear immediately but from now on, mine was a victorious march, ever onward. When I started chanting the Hare Krishna mahamantra, as I have mentioned earlier, I was filled with so much energy that all the darkness within, which had been muzzling my natural flair for public speaking, had no choice but to leave, and a day would dawn when I would snivel no longer, roaring with my mighty voice as I always had done.

There are two episodes that come to mind when I was still seeking redemption from my travails.

Some people wanted to enter into a partnership with me and gave me a lucrative offer that I quickly accepted. But then, I was supposed to attract students to our prep center, and they came up with the idea that I address a huge gathering of prospective students at a reputed engineering college, "Look, you're an authority in your subject and would be the best person to convince these kids why they should come to us," they said, much to my horror. "I'm finding it so difficult to talk to a handful of students in my class and that is why I prefer small batches. How will I address so many!" I thought, trembling.

But there was no way I could back out, and I'd to go. The night before, I was so disturbed—Something terrible will definitely happen, some terrible physical harm! The morning inevitably came, and I steeled myself. As soon as I entered the auditorium, I invoked Krishna and spoke. It was amazing—I was my old self, the champion debater, the brilliant actor with that deep voice and confident swagger. I was riding my instinct, and everyone was spellbound. Students were literally eating out of my hands, and it was such a glorious feeling. I loved myself that day. That warmth of confidence, that feeling of strength—this is what I'd yearned for years. No longer the weak, sniveling cowardice that I hated so much. Even though there was not much financial outcome due to several other factors, it was a huge personal triumph.

Shortly after, some parents requested me to meet them and at stake was a big batch. It meant good money, but it also meant I'd have to talk to many parents at the same time. I somehow managed with kids as they were my students eager to learn, and I was the tutor highly respected for my knowledge. They would find me odd for sure, but I would hide behind the widely held notion that geniuses were eccentrics—I hope I'm a genius—but, nonetheless, a convenient getaway was up for grabs, and I'd breathe a bit easy. But parents were a different ball game. They would ask so many questions and were so hard to convince. Worst of all, they appeared so threatening to my fragile psyche. I tried hard to avoid them, but they'd heard so many good things about me that it was impossible to shake them off. Then I watched a movie centered around Krishna, showing He protected and guided an ignorant soul who was then redeemed from his dishonest ways. And here I was, his ardent devotee. Surely nothing could hurt me, thought I and then resolved to meet those parents. The meeting was a success and not only did I get a big batch but also references from some of the parents because they were so happy.

Fear limits you. Imagine a life that you can live on your own terms—if you wish to shut your eyes and sit calmly for as long as you wish, you can. You can laugh, you can sing, do whatever as per your sweet will. Nothing limits you. How wonderful would it be to live life on your own terms! But we limit ourselves because we are so scared—What people would think? I might look like a fool. If you're scared, people get the license to bully you—ask those timid school kids. It could very well threaten your life too, as it happened in my case. So just say no to fear—all justifications for fear may rot in hell! It's your biggest enemy; offer it no scope or you'll be caught in a spiral and find it so hard to escape. Nip it in the bud. Anything that limits a perfectly normal activity by threatening you in vague terms is poison. Root it out there and then and see how beautiful life can be. Fear is always vague; it will limit you by whispering in your ear—Something bad will happen if you do this. But it will never be clear what evil would follow. When you stop, it will threaten you more, and you stop again, and then it will spin a web of deceit that will be so hard to break out of. Do what fear asks you not to do, and keep on doing the same, and fear will cringe away because it never had any substance in the first place. It only bluffs. Call that bluff calmly. If you agitate, you'll scatter your energies, and it will be harder to destroy fear. So be calm whatever the provocation and persevere till fear is extinguished.

CHAPTER THIRTY

Life was not always unkind. I had money to spend and because I worked seven days a week the whole year, I planned getaways in the city itself, and a friend suggested a five-star hotel for short stays. My wife and I would stay there, and I would feel proud to offer her such luxury. The hotel had fantastic food, and we would just laze—my wife would not need to cook and just order whatever she wished, and I felt so happy, "She has gone through so much without complaining and now, by the grace of Krishna, I can offer her what those fiendish relatives of ours, who tormented us so much just because we had no money, can't even dream of." Most of our married life we had suffered utter deprivation, but now, it was our time, and no one could deprive us of anything, any more. I truly believe and will believe forever—This is Krishna. All this luxury is His grace, and we will enjoy this bliss forever. When I bought a beautiful car, I never felt I owned it. It was something gifted by Krishna because He felt I deserved some comfort. We would buy expensive stuff, and none of us stopped the other one because we'd suffered utter penury for so long.

I met interesting characters among my students, and I would like to discuss two of them.

One was the daughter of this tycoon who had been crazily rich through generations. Ash was a good student and very humble. But she was depressed too. It's difficult to figure out why. She looked good, respected her elders, worked out in the gym, and had no bad habits. But then she'd been bullied in her school—I'd been bullied too but luckily, did not end up getting depressed. Maybe she was too sensitive but whatever the reason, she'd an instant connect with me. She grew so fond of me that she revealed a lot, "Sir, I was administered anti-depressants that are prescribed only to adults. When we consulted some doctors in New York, they stopped my medicines forthwith, and I blanked out. For some days, I could remember nothing. I was so fearful that I couldn't bear to see my reflection in the mirror, and the servants had to cover all the mirrors in the house with cloth."

I was really touched, "Look, I've been through a terrible phase myself. But the solution lies in faith, not fear. With my belief in Krishna, I'm stable and calm, no longer tossed around helplessly by uncontrollable thoughts. My medicines are being tapered off too." "So, what do I do," she asked desperately, and there was so much pain in her voice. "Surrender totally to Him. Let Him take care. Your power is finite, but His grace is infinite and nothing limits Him. He will take care as He has done in my case," I said with so much of conviction. She broke down in tears and decided to try out this piece of advice. She was much calmer later and went on to do great things in life on her own, and I feel so proud when I read about her in the newspapers.

I know for sure that divine help is the real thing but even if you're a non-believer, give it a try. You're fearful because you're insecure. When you believe there's someone taking care, that you're not alone, you feel safe and become tranquil. When this happens, fear vanishes. But when you try to take the burden upon yourself, it's really tough. Maybe the strong-willed can survive tough times without much ado, but those with fragile mental states cannot bear the stress—I know this first-hand. So, we need some assurance and if we believe that someone can take care of anything that threatens us, we feel safe.

So, all of you feeling helpless and crushed, seek God and believe me, faith works wonders.

The other student, Katie, was the child of a very rich man too, but definitely way below the league of the girl I just talked about. What she talked of was money and money alone. Anyone not rich by her standards was not worth her attention. I once casually asked her, "What do you think drives me?" I thought she would respect my intellect and say some nice things. But I was in for humiliation, "Why should I bother, you're just a teacher." Then some more nuggets of wisdom, "The car you drive is so cheap. My drivers drive such cars." And which driver affords a sedan in India, may I ask! There was yet another brilliant piece when I showed her the picture of a student of mine who went to MIT, no less, "Her bag is so shabby," and then the horror, "She looks pregnant." Now, this student of mine was so fit and not pregnant at all. It was sheer jealousy because she had such lousy grades. And she would be so appreciative of this other student of mine who was as bad as her at studies and a drug addict just because he was the son of a tycoon.

Not only Katie, most of the kids from affluent families don't really bother about you beyond their lessons and when you're as full of ideas as I am, you really feel hurt. I not only discuss academics but also life but then, I am troubled by this nagging doubt—Do they really care? My wife tells me, "Limit yourself to academics. Do not preach because no one really cares. Why do you want to suffer rejection unnecessarily?" But I can't; I must go beyond because, to me, the kid must gain from what life has taught me and not commit the same mistakes that made my life so insufferable.

There were other reasons too that made me feel, at times, that teaching was largely a thankless job in my city even though it had given me all the things I yearned for all my life and that my wife always pointed out I should be thankful for. Whenever a student excelled, he would say, in most cases, "I was super smart and never needed any teacher." His parents would exult, "It's in his DNA! Our family is so smart." The mothers would credit their husbands, even if they were not well-educated, with all the prep. If someone did badly, it was of course the teacher who was so incompetent. In such cases, the parents never prepped their kids at all. Also, in many cases in Mumbai, neither the parents nor the kids would pick up your call once the results were out, irrespective of how the child fared. One such mother removed me as a friend on a popular social medium the moment she learned her son had done very well.

CHAPTER THIRTY-ONE

Meeting my relatives at weddings was very therapeutic. At my niece's wedding in Delhi, I was with my brothers and sister and a host of others after a very long time. Loaded with work, I'd no time to venture out of Mumbai. How suffocating that had been I realized when I was among so many relatives at the same time. At first, I was scared because I would need to talk to so many people, but my younger brother greeted me so warmly that my fear ebbed. And then so many people were talking—no room for hesitation, no escape route at all—and I just let myself go. There was no need to coax myself into composure either. My instinct just took over, and I marveled at the fluency with which I was talking.

I had my reservations about the kind of accommodation and the quality of drinking water too—Mumbai was my comfort zone as many a time I would be eating at five-star hotels and staying there too for short vacays. But the accommodation here was modest, the food from not-too-great caterers, and I was fearful—something bad would certainly happen, my stomach would definitely be infected, and so on. But then I let go of myself, and it was such a fantastic experience, people laughing, poking fun and all that, and my circumscribed life would be free, and it was all so magical.

Sometimes I wonder why I'm fearful whenever I've to step out of my comfort zone. Maybe I'm scared that I will lose everything if I fall sick—I've been through so much in life, and I shudder at the thought of that poverty. But the way out is through fear, not rotting under limits. And if you cannot enjoy now, when will you? There's no other time than now, and the worst thing is to grow old and then rue—Oh, only if I'd shown some courage then! And that time will never come back, the time when you could have laughed and been happy.

At yet another wedding, my nephew's, I again had to talk non-stop to so many relatives who had no idea about my problem. And again, I let myself go because there was no alternative, and things were fine. And then there was this French girl I met who casually said, "You talk about phobia. What phobia? I never had any," and I was incredulous—Oh my God, how amazing, how wonderful! Here's a girl who doesn't even know what phobia is and just look at me!

Please remember that this was the time when I had not started chanting the Hare Krishna mahamantra and was not totally aligned with Krishna and hence, fearful. This would change dramatically when I would be firmly positioned in the Krishna mindset and awash with His Light.

Even though we didn't have our own kids, some babies chose to fill our lives with their warmth. One of them, Janie, was in the same building as us, and one evening, as I was alighting from a cab, she came rushing and just wrapped herself around my knees. I later learned that she used to call out to me from her window when I was taking a walk, but I never paid attention. She was just one year old then. She would then become an integral part of our family, and I would grow so fond of her. We loved to buy her gifts though she never demanded any. My wife bought her a pink frock and a wand, and she looked so pretty, a fairy indeed. Many a time I would wake up to find her on my bed—my wife loved to do all this. And then, her parents had to shift because their landlord refused to extend their lease. It was a crushing blow, and I was so depressed. I would come home in the night from work and would not see her in her window and feel terrible. It was at this time that I suffered this terrible blow during a meeting I discussed earlier that froze my nerves, threatened my life, and almost destroyed my career. I would love babies later but would not get so terribly attached as in this case.

And then there was another baby, Paddy, the son of my wife's cousin. I was very strongly attached to my mother and her death left me devastated. How could she go like this—Didn't I entrust her to Krishna and didn't she promise she would come again the next summer? How could fate be so cruel, snatching her away just like that? Then this lady got pregnant, and somehow, I got the feeling that the baby was my mother taking a new birth because she'd been so sick. I was fond of taking my mother to five-star hotels because she loved such luxuries and wonder of wonders, when my wife and I booked a suite at such a hotel, the baby was the first one to occupy our bed and sleep so blissfully. It so happened that his parents visited us the same day we checked in, and I was away for work when my wife messaged me this adorable piece of news. The baby is very fond of us, and so are we. It's again interesting that the first time I shopped for a baby, it was for him. What a coincidence, and how fulfilled I felt because how else would've I shopped for a baby as I've no kids of my own.

Strangely, I was never so attached to my elder brother's daughter, Izzy, who'd been intruding into our lives as a toddler when we were just married. She would be after us the whole day when we were visiting Patna and would even go out with us. I would be driving my brother's scooter, my wife riding pillion, and this toddler would stand in front of me, in the narrow space just beyond my seat, singing a song with an elaborate movement of her hands. I only know how difficult it was to balance that scooter, but she would not listen and accompany us invariably. Even in the night, she would sneak into our bedroom. I would be shutting the door when my wife would tease, "See, who's in," and my romantic ideas would go for a toss.

Not only her, I was generally not attached to any kid at that time while my wife loved them. Maybe the subconscious knew I wouldn't have kids and since I'd never been very involved, the pain was less.

Let me now tell you a bit about my elder brother again, whom I met after a long time at my nephew's wedding. I got to talk to him a lot as we were sharing the same suite, a suite in name alone, in a very ordinary hotel. I was quite impressed by his positivity—here was a man who was facing so much trouble but would not think anything negative even for a moment. His wife was seriously ill; he was not earning much; and his children were pretty young with little sense of responsibility. He was doing well as a bank officer, but then his enemies got the better of him, and he was slapped with compulsory retirement on trumped-up charges. Not to be put down so easily and choosing to fight, he filed a case against the bank, seeking his reinstatement. The pension he was given was measly, and he had a daughter to marry and two sons to settle—the boys were still studying. He had to get a job to meet the expenses, and he left no stone unturned till he landed a decent job, though not very lucrative. However, his pension and the salary from this job were just about enough for him to discharge his responsibilities. He got his daughter married to a nice guy, and things seemed to look good. But then his wife was diagnosed with a serious ailment that kept on getting worse. His in-laws and other relatives from his wife's side were most disinterested and insulting, even calling him a parasite because he requested them to help. Come to think of it, his wife, after all, is their own daughter, and it doesn't hurt to help one their own.

As a result, he had to take care of his wife, who could not even move, do all household chores, from cleaning and washing clothes to heating and serving food, buying vegetables and fruits, standing in serpentine queues to get money out of ATMs, and so on, besides travelling by even buses and local trains to do a full-time job that demanded constant attention. And his kids were of so little help, lost in their private worlds. "They do not understand my age, they feel as if I'm still twenty-six years old," he blurted out.

What I admire is his courage—he won't quit, be it fighting for his reinstatement or wrestling with his circumstances. He would always be positive, that he would win, that things would turn out just fine. I see in him the same fighting spirit that my father had. Even the circumstances are eerily similar—my father, too, had lost his job and had young children to take care of. My brother, though, is much healthier despite his diabetes and blood pressure. He's just so full of energy and optimism that his children forget he has some daunting diseases too.

I sometimes felt quite stupid talking to him about petty fears that dogged me, such as how clean the drinking water and the food in the hotel were. My brother advised, "Look at the bigger picture. Life is so much more. Don't get bogged down by insignificant things." And I would feel reassured.

CHAPTER THIRTY-TWO

Travelling by air had an ennobling effect on me. When my mother died in Patna, I caught a flight to pay her my respects, and I was flying after a really long time. It also was the first flight I'd paid for from my own pocket and in normal circumstances, I would've felt really proud—air travel is considered elite in India. I was a bit scared but also thrilled when the aircraft galloped at full throttle before the take-off. Once in the air at thirty-five thousand feet, I felt very philosophical—on the ground, we suffer so many petty fears, but here one mishap could wipe out our very lives. I was not fearful at all—I was feeling very close to Krishna, surrendering everything to Him. If He wished so, I was willing to go to Him, and if He wanted me to stay in this world a little longer, that was also okay with me. When the plane hit bad weather and was shaking, the crew asking us to fasten our seat belts, I was calm, the only botheration being that the tea I was sipping might spill over! Then I felt I had enough of this bad weather and told Krishna—Please set the plane right. I want to enjoy my tea. Can you believe it, the weather cleared, the plane steadied, and we were soon allowed to unfasten our seat belts.

When I alighted, I was so confident and thrilled that I forgot the pain of the loss for some time, feeling—Yes, I've lost my mother, but I've Krishna with me.

Another experience with Krishna happened in Delhi when I was visiting for my nephew's engagement. I started late for my flight back home, and Delhi traffic is terrible. The cabbie was blunt, "You'd never reach the airport in time. When I tell you, you get down and catch a metro to reach faster." I debated the idea and found it too bothersome to alight with all the luggage, catch an escalator, go all the way down to the metro, board it with all my luggage, and then alight at a station near the airport. I would then need to get out of the station and catch a cab to reach the airport. Way too much trouble! I then told Krishna I needed to reach in time and instructed the taxi driver to take me straight to the airport. I was at the airport much before I'd to check in and would always remember the lesson—Do not fear and leave the matter to Krishna. He will take care of everything.

So, what is the greatest lesson I've learnt from my, well, a rather unusual life? Absolute, total faith in God, absolute, total surrender to His will. Believe me, when you do that, bliss only follows because God loves us and does the best we are entitled to. Why did I suffer so much, it's hard to tell. But what is very clear is that I faced my toughest challenges when I was without God. First, Lord Hanuman came into my life, and I rose like a meteor, and you all know that. Wasn't it a miracle that someone so disorganized as I was became so focused, so energetic that only a great life seemed imminent? Then, I faltered in my faith due to whatever reasons and my life went for a toss. Fear froze me, and I committed blunder after blunder. I'm sure I would have been telling you a different story had I not lost faith, because faith was my power and without God, I was a plaything of fate or whatever else you call the forces beyond your control. Even after my father's death, when I seemed to have gotten rid of my confusion, I was not actually back to my absolute faith, engaging in rituals only. Mere rituals are never enough—it's the deep spiritual connection that matters whether you observe any ritual or not. And yes, I was forced out of Lord Hanuman during the darkest phase of my life. Maybe it was an ordeal by fire to test how much I was one with God. Maybe it was a conspiracy to propel me towards the Supreme Lord, Shri Krishna. I'm saying again—Lord Hanuman could not have done a more blissful thing for me if it were His design to let me enter Krishna's grace. And with Krishna, I've found fulfillment. I now feel so powerful that it seems I can literally soar into the sky, jump across mountains. When I'm full of Him, it's a panacea—nothing, nothing at all, can harm me. My psychiatric medicines are almost over; my orthopedist told me my arm was fine and I could do gym again, and I am building that fab physique again—girls swooned over it while guys died of envy, remember? I'm full of courage and really calm. See how beautiful it is—I suffered so much because I was so fearful, but now I can analyze challenges very calmly because I know Krishna protects me at all times. My energies are not scattered at all, and I'm able to overcome hurdles so well. I toss fears aside so nonchalantly that I'm myself surprised. Gone is that sniveling cowardice that I hated so much and yes, I can converse so well, pulling myself to my full height, all of my six feet, and looking the world straight in the eye. Where is the space for chills of any kind when you are so full of Krishna's warmth! And yes, I manifest with a pure heart what I really desire and Krishna grants my wishes so many times!

So, where do I stand now? In the abode of heavenly bliss—extremely positive, vibrant, full of life. Gone are the days of pain, deprivation, and failure. Persist I must and I do with faith that no more shall I suffer. And Lord Hanuman is by my side while Lord Krishna drives my chariot through the ocean of life that was so turbulent once, its waves leaping high with hunger to devour my very life, but is so tranquil now, so much at peace, and I feel invincible.

The sun shines after a long, dark night,
And wings full of Krishna,
I soar beyond,
Beyond limits,
Beyond the realms of plausibility,
Into the bliss divine that Krishna designed
For this dear son of His!

ACKNOWLEDGEMENTS

My dear father, you were a multifaceted genius, a powerhouse of talent that one rarely comes across in life. Learned a lot from you, including the art of writing. My dear mother, I salute your courage that you so nonchalantly displayed amidst tremendous odds. My dear wife, Usha, I don't know what I would have done in life had it not been for your prescience and unwavering support. My father would have been proud of you! Dear parents-in-law, thanks so much for what you did for me. Myesha and Ridhhaan, you two have been real bundles of joy, lighting up Usha's and my life!

Nothing could parallel your grace, Hanuman Ji! You miraculously transformed my life when I was a lost teenager, blessing me with health, intellect, and vitality and have been my Supreme Protector all my life!

About the Author

The author is an elite tutor preparing students for American standardised tests, sending the best of them to such esteemed seats of learning as MIT, Stanford, Harvard, Princeton, Yale and more! Having taught for more than two decades, he has come across a rich mosaic of life, all of which he has woven into an engrossing tale, depicting the ascension from darkness of fear to sheer bliss by the grace of Krishna, the Writer of the writer's existence and beyond!